E

THE ELEPHANT
and other funny stories

EGBERT
THE ELEPHANT
and other funny stories

Edited by Barbara Ireson

Illustrated by Jon Miller

CORGI BOOKS

EGBERT THE ELEPHANT AND
OTHER FUNNY STORIES

A CORGI BOOK 0 552 52413 1

First publication in Great Britain

PRINTING HISTORY
Corgi edition published 1987
Corgi edition reprinted 1987

Collection copyright © Barbara Ireson 1987
Illustrations copyright © Jon Miller 1987

This book is set in 12/14 pt Century Schoolbook
by Colset Private Limited, Singapore

Corgi Books are published by Transworld Publishers
Ltd., 61–63 Uxbridge Road, Ealing, London W5 5SA,
in Australia by Transworld Publishers (Australia)
Pty. Ltd., 15–23 Helles Avenue, Moorebank, NSW
2170, and in New Zealand by Transworld Publishers
(N.Z.) Ltd., Cnr. Moselle and Waipareira Avenues,
Henderson, Auckland.

Reproduced, printed and bound in Great Britain by
Hazell Watson & Viney Limited,
Member of the BPCC Group,
Aylesbury, Bucks

Acknowledgements

EGBERT THE ELEPHANT by Harold Zahorik
Reprinted from *The Wishing Penny and Other Fantasy Stories* published by Parents Magazine Press. Every effort has been made to trace the copyright holder of this story.

DID I EVER TELL YOU ABOUT THE TERRIBLE THING MARGARET DID ON HER FIRST DAY AT SCHOOL by Iris Grender
Reprinted from *Did I ever Tell You . . .* Reproduced by permission of Century Hutchinson Publishing Group Ltd.

PHILBERT THE FEARFUL by Jay Williams
Reprinted from *The Practical Princess and Other Liberating Fairy Tales*. Reproduced by permission of The Bodley Head Ltd.

THE DRIBBLESOME TEAPOTS by Norman Hunter
Reprinted from *The Dribblesome Teapots* by Norman Hunter, reproduced by permission of The Bodley Head Ltd.

HARE TAKES MR KNOWALL BADGER DOWN A PEG OR TWO by Elizabeth Robinson
Copyright © Elizabeth Robinson 1987

SEND THREE AND FOURPENCE WE ARE GOING TO A DANCE by Jan Mark
Reprinted from *Nothing to Be Afraid of* by Jan Mark (Kestrel Books, 1980), pp 98–107, copyright

Contents

Egbert the Elephant

Harold Zahorik

Egbert was a plaid elephant who lived in the playroom with the mohair lion and the rubber mouse.

One night, after everyone had gone to bed, Egbert wandered out of the playroom and down the hall to see what there was to see. He wandered into the kitchen, where he sniffed at the cupboards. Everything smelled quite delicious, but since a plaid elephant is full of stuffing, he wasn't hungry.

From the cupboards he waddled over to a round box in the corner. It didn't look very interesting until a little grey head poked itself over the top.

'Hello,' said Egbert the elephant.

'Hello,' said the little grey head. The little grey head was really a part of the little grey mouse, but Egbert couldn't see the rest of him because he was in the waste basket.

'Who are you?' asked the mouse.

'I'm . . . I'm . . . I don't remember,' said Egbert.

'You don't remember?' said the mouse.

'I don't remember,' repeated Egbert. 'I don't remember much of anything.'

'Let me look at you,' said the mouse. 'I know what you are. You're an elephant.'

'Yes, that's what I am,' said Egbert. 'I'm an . . . what you said I was.'

'An elephant,' repeated the mouse.

'An elephant,' repeated Egbert.

'And do you know what I am?' asked the mouse.

'I don't even remember what I am,' said Egbert. And he didn't.

'You are an elephant,' said the mouse slowly. 'I am a mouse. And do you know what elephants are afraid of more than anything?'

'What?' asked Egbert.

'Elephants are afraid of mice,' said the mouse.

'They are?' asked Egbert.

'They are,' said the mouse. 'And I am a mouse. You are afraid of me.'

'I must remember that,' said Egbert, but he wasn't sure that he could.

The little mouse disappeared into the waste basket, and Egbert waddled into another room. This room was filled with books, and they all looked at Egbert as he entered. It was rather strange to have an elephant in the library even if he was only

11

eight and three-quarter inches high.

'Who are you?' asked the telephone book.

'Who . . . me?' asked Egbert.

'Of course,' said the phone book. 'Your name, please.'

'I don't remember,' said Egbert.

'You don't remember!' exclaimed the appointment book who never forgot anything.

'I don't remember,' said Egbert.

'From your general appearance, which is somewhat unusual, I would judge you to be an elephant,' said the encyclopaedia. He was very wise.

'I remember,' said Egbert. 'I am either an elephant or a mouse. If I am an elephant, I am afraid of a mouse. On the other hand, I may be a mouse, and if I am a mouse, then I believe I am afraid of elephants. Dear me, I do wish I could remember which I am.'

'Without a doubt, you are an elephant,' said the encyclopaedia.

It was then that the mohair lion walked into the room looking for Egbert. When Egbert spied him, he rushed across the room and lay trembling under the desk.

'What is the matter with you?' asked the mohair lion.

'Are you a mouse?' asked Egbert cautiously.

'I am a lion,' said the lion. 'I have told you a hundred times. I am a lion. You are an elephant, and elephants are afraid of mice, not lions.'

'Oh, yes,' said Egbert, coming out from under the desk. 'I must remember that.'

'I just don't understand you,' said the mohair lion. 'An elephant is never supposed to forget anything, but you just don't remember.'

'It does seem very hard for me to remember things,' said Egbert.

'But it isn't hard at all,' said the appointment book. 'I remember when things are supposed to be done.'

'I remember names and addresses, to say nothing of telephone numbers,' added the telephone book.

'I remember the meaning of words,' said the dictionary.

'And I remember anything about everything,' said the encyclopaedia.

'And that gives me an idea,' said the mohair lion.

As Egbert looked on, the mohair lion jumped on to the bookshelf and spoke quietly with each book. The books smiled as he talked to them.

'We think it is a fine idea,' they all said together.

'Then we'll do it right now,' said the mohair lion. And he began. First, he nipped a small corner of a page from each of the books. It bothered them a little, but they were happy to help the little elephant. When he had collected all the bits of paper, the mohair lion walked over to Egbert. 'The trouble with you is that stuffing in your head. Your brain is fuzzy. Now sit still.' Egbert sat still and the mohair lion began stuffing bits of paper into the elephant's head through a tiny hole where the sewing had come apart. 'There,' he said when he had finished. 'Now you have in your head a little of what each of these books remembers.'

'What is your name?' asked the phone book.

'Egbert,' said Egbert.

'What are you?' asked the encyclopaedia.

'An elephant,' answered Egbert the elephant.

'Wonderful,' said the mohair lion, and at that very moment the little rubber mouse entered the room. 'Hello,' he said.

Egbert began to tremble. He lumbered and stumbled and tumbled across the room and ended up with just his plaid trunk sticking out from beneath the desk.

'What's the matter with him?' asked the rubber mouse.

The books and the mohair lion laughed and laughed.

'At last, Egbert is an elephant,' said the mohair lion. 'I don't think he will ever forget again.'

And he didn't.

Did I Ever Tell You About the Terrible Thing Margaret Did on Her First Day at School?

Iris Grender

When we started school our mothers dressed us in new clothes from top to toe. We had new coats, new shoes, new socks, new skirts, new blouses, new jumpers and even new vests and pants.

We had our names sewn into our clothes to keep them from being muddled up with the clothes of other children. So we were all new children with brand-new clothes.

When my friend Margaret went into
school her mother said, 'Just mind you
don't lose anything, and have a nice time.'
So Margaret decided to be extra careful to
look after all her things.

We hadn't been in school long when a
button fell off Margaret's brand-new
blouse. She picked the button up from the
floor. She knew it was very important not
to lose the button. Somehow Margaret
would have to mind the button all day
long until her mother could sew it back on.

Margaret looked for somewhere safe to

keep the button. She put it into her shoe but it hurt. So she took it out again.

Then she did a terrible thing with the button. Margaret knew that children must never put things into their ears or their mouths. But she didn't know that they must never put things up their noses.

So Margaret stuffed the button up her nose to keep it safe.

Soon her nose began to turn red. The button was hurting it. She tried to get the button out. It was stuck.

Margaret went out to Miss White, the teacher. 'My button's hurting me,' she said. Miss White looked at the buttons on Margaret's blouse.

'I can't think why they should be,' she answered. Of course, Miss White couldn't see the button stuck in Margaret's nose.

'It's the button I'm keeping safe inside my nose that's hurting,' said Margaret. She was beginning to cry by this time.

Miss White tried to get the button out with a tissue. We all watched. And we all thought, School is a very interesting place!

Then Margaret went to the head-mistress. She couldn't get the button out either. Then the headmistress sent for

Margaret's mother.

They went to the hospital. A doctor and two nurses managed to get the precious button out of Margaret's nose.

So Margaret went to school, for the first time, and to hospital, for the first time, all in one day.

On her second day at school Margaret was very careful not to do anything terrible. She showed us the famous button. It was sewn on very firmly. And so were the other buttons on her blouse.

Philbert the Fearful

Jay Williams

Sir Philbert Fitzhugh was not very brave. This wouldn't have mattered had he been a merchant or a mason or a mouse-catcher, but he was a knight. Other knights were riding out to slay dragons or rescue princesses, but Sir Philbert stayed comfortably at home taking care of his health, curled up by the fire with a good book and an apple.

'After all,' he said, 'I am the only one of me I have, and I have to take care of myself.'

Everyone said, 'Knights ought to be

brave as lions.'

'Maybe so,' replied Sir Philbert. 'But *I* think it's more important to keep your health.' And he went back to his reading and his fire and his apple. 'An apple a day,' he added, 'keeps the doctor away.'

Nevertheless, the doctor came one day and had dinner, and he poked Sir Philbert in the chest and looked at his tongue and felt his pulse. Then he shook his head.

'You're getting flabby,' he said sternly. 'Look at yourself! You're pale. You've got the beginnings of a potbelly. I recommend

a long trip and a change of scene.'

'But I get homesick,' Sir Philbert protested.

The doctor snorted. 'Fiddlesticks! Tomorrow morning,' said he, 'three bold knights are going to search for the Emperor's daughter, who has been kidnapped by an enchanter named Brasilgore. I order you to go with them. The adventure will be the best thing for you.'

The next morning at half-past four, the three bold knights started out on their quest. With them was a fourth knight, not so bold. It was Sir Philbert.

He had plenty of warm blankets rolled up behind his saddle. He had plenty of food and medicine in his saddlebags. But he was far from happy.

The other three knights, however, were perfectly happy. They were named Sir Hugo of Brandish, Sir Armet of Anguish, and Sir Brian of Thump. Their armour was rusty and dented from many adventures. In their saddlebags they carried nothing but bread and hard cheese. Their moustaches were as fierce as their talk.

'We'll slay Brasilgore the enchanter, and find the Emperor's daughter, or die in the attempt!' roared Sir Brian.

'Then I certainly hope we find her,'

mumbled Sir Philbert.

They travelled for many days until they came to a wide, sad plain. Nothing grew there but twisted thorn bushes and purple heather. A wind from the north blew steadily over it. They rode and rode through the heather and into the wind, and at noon they came to a tower. It was high and black. It had one window at the top and a door in front which was a good deal higher than a house.

As they gazed up at it, wondering what it was for, a maiden put her head out of the window.

'Help, help!' she cried.

Sir Brian shaded his eyes. 'Are you a prisoner?' he called.

'Yes, I am. Please go away,' said the maiden.

'Eh?' Sir Brian looked puzzled. 'But you just said, "Help, help".'

'Oh, dear, I know I did. I'm sorry. I said, "Help, help", but I meant go away.'

'But why?' asked Sir Hugo of Brandish.

Just then the enormous door opened. 'That's why,' said the maiden. 'Alas, alas, this is the end of you. Goodbye.'

Out stepped a giant a good deal higher than a house. He drew a deep breath, stretched, and yawned. It sounded like a thunderstorm overhead.

Sir Hugo lowered his lance. 'Stand back, all of you,' he shouted. 'This giant is mine!'

He rode straight at the giant's ankle and thrust his lance.

'Oh, well done,' said Sir Brian.

The giant uttered a yell, 'Hornets!' He stamped his foot angrily. Sir Hugo disappeared.

'Adventures!' groaned Sir Philbert. 'I just wish that rotten doctor were here.'

The other two knights stared uneasily at each other and then at the giant who was grumbling like an earthquake.

Sir Philbert quickly unfastened his big roll of blankets. He shook them out. He turned his horse and began to gallop away, letting the blankets stream behind him like banners.

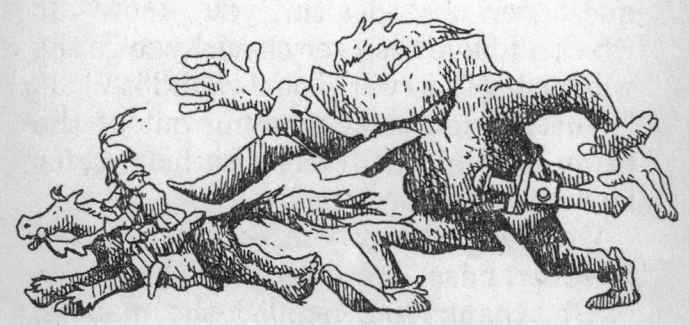

The giant saw Sir Philbert and made a giant stride to smash him. Sir Philbert let go of the blankets. They blew away in the endless wind. They flew up and plastered themselves over the giant's eyes. He missed his footing, stumbled on a rock, and fell on his head with a crash. Since he was so much bigger and heavier than an ordinary person, he fell with a far bigger and heavier crash. It was the end of him.

Sir Armet and Sir Brian trotted over and stared at the giant's body. They shook their heads.

'Listen,' said Sir Armet, 'I don't think that was very sporting.'

'It was nothing but an accident,' Sir Brian agreed. 'Philbert didn't kill the giant. He killed himself.'

'Yes, I suppose he did,' said Sir Philbert. He opened his helmet and mopped his forehead. 'But I came on this quest for my health, you know. It wouldn't have been very healthy to go the way poor Hugo went, now would it?'

The maiden came running out of the tower. Sir Philbert took off his helmet, for he was always very polite.

'I'm glad to say you are no longer a prisoner, miss,' he said.

'Oh, thank you,' smiled the maiden,

who had large, merry brown eyes and long brown hair in two plaits down her back. 'I'll just get my things, if you'll wait a minute.'

'What?' huffed Sir Brian. 'Get your things?'

'Of course. I'm coming with you. You rescued me, didn't you?'

'You can't come with us,' said Sir Armet. 'It's much too dangerous.'

'Besides, we haven't an extra horse,' said Sir Brian.

'She can ride with me,' Sir Philbert said.

The maiden smiled at him. She ran into the tower and soon returned with four large bundles. They hung the bundles on Sir Philbert's horse, and Sir Philbert said it was just as well his blankets had all blown away. Then the maiden — whose name was Victoria — got up behind, and away they rode once more.

Victoria said, 'I was watching from the window. Did you really expect those blankets to fly up over the giant's face?'

Sir Philbert sighed. 'I hoped so,' he said.

'If they hadn't, what would you have done?'

'I would have kept on riding as fast as I could. I didn't see how else I could beat a giant that tall.'

'But shouldn't a knight be brave?'

'Oh, yes,' said Sir Philbert. 'But on the other hand, I'm the only one of me I have, and I have to take care of myself.'

Victoria nodded. 'That's reasonable,' she said.

They rode on. At last they came to a high place. The road ran over a peak that sparkled with glassy ice. On each side, the rock fell away in steep cliffs, down, down, to glittering rock below. Sir Brian's horse suddenly reared and skittered around. Sir Armet's horse reared too. After a bit Sir Philbert and Victoria caught up with them and saw what they saw. Their horse couldn't rear because it was too heavily loaded.

There was a cockatrice in the way. It had the body of a serpent and the head and legs of a cockerel. Its scales were green and shiny in the icy light. Its long serpent tongue flicked in and out of its cock's beak, and its round, evil eyes rolled forward to look at them. It strutted as tall as a man.

'Hmm,' said Sir Philbert. 'It might be better to go back and find another way. After all, we have a lady with us.'

'Pah! You are a coward, sir,' said Sir

Armet. 'Stand back, all of you.'

He lowered his lance and galloped forward.

'Oh dear!' Sir Philbert whispered to Victoria.

Sir Armet's lance shattered on the green scales. The cockatrice hissed. Its beak darted fowards on its snaky neck. Sir Armet's horse gave a scream and plunged over the edge of the cliff with Sir Armet.

'Stand back, all of you,' said Sir Brian nervously. He began to lower his lance. But Sir Philbert caught his elbow.

'Wait a minute,' said Sir Philbert. 'I just thought of something I'd like to try.'

He got off his horse. 'Victoria my dear,' he said, 'have you a mirror?'

'Oh, yes,' she answered. She opened one of her bundles and took out a large, golden looking-glass with her initial 'V' in emeralds on the back.

Sir Philbert took it and walked forward, his armour squeaking and clinking in the still, cold air. The cockatrice shot out its fearsome head once again. Sir Philbert held out the mirror.

The cockatrice stared into it. Then it gave a dithering hiss of horror, spread its wings, and flew away over the peaks.

Sir Philbert returned the looking-glass to Victoria. He was shaking like a leaf.

'Why, how brave of you!' cried Victoria, giving him a hug.

'No, not very brave,' said Sir Philbert. 'The only thing a cockatrice is afraid of is another cockatrice. I was pretty sure it would fly off when it saw its face in the mirror. I read that in a book,' he added humbly.

'Then it was very clever of you,' Victoria said firmly.

'Humph!' grunted Sir Brian. 'Clever? I'm not so sure a knight *ought* to be clever.'

Sir Philbert hung his head. 'I know. But you see, I'm the only one of me I have . . .'

'Suppose we have a bite of lunch and then push on,' Sir Brian said briskly.

When they had finished eating, they followed the road over the top of the mountain and down the other side. After a time, Sir Philbert remarked, 'These trees are growing in rows, almost like a park.'

'Rubbish!' said Sir Brian. 'It's a wild wood.'

'There's no undergrowth either,' Sir Philbert continued.

'Ridiculous!' said Sir Brian. 'Next

you'll be telling me you see a castle.'

'I see a castle,' Sir Philbert said.

Sure enough, the trees ended at a bridge, and on the other side of it there was a gloomy castle with many turrets.

'Ha!' Sir Brian exclaimed. 'The castle of the enchanter!'

'Are you sure?' asked Sir Philbert.

'Of course I'm sure. Don't you think I know what an enchanter's castle looks like?' Sir Brian retorted.

They rode across the bridge and under a gateway like a giant's yawn, into a paved courtyard. All was silent.

Sir Brian rubbed his hands together. 'Now then,' he said. 'The enchanter is probably upstairs in his den. I'll go after him. If anything happens to me — which isn't very likely because I know how to handle these fellows — just remember one rule. You must hold on to the enchanter until he surrenders. He will turn himself into all sorts of beasts: a lion, a wolf, a dragon, anything. As long as you hold him you're safe. If you let go of him, he'll magic you, and — *poof*!'

Sir Philbert nodded. 'I've read all about that in —' he began, but Sir Brian was gone.

Sir Philbert rubbed his chin. 'You

know,' he said to Victoria, 'I'm not at all sure this is the right castle.'

'Never mind,' said Victoria.

'But I *do* mind. I think I'd better follow Brian. Suppose something happens to him?'

'Suppose something happens to you?' said Victoria.

'Don't let's talk about it,' Sir Philbert gulped.

He walked into the castle. There was a large cobwebby hall with a winding, dusty stair at one end of it. He could see Sir Brian's footprints in the dust. He began to follow them.

Now Sir Brian had climbed the stairs, and he had found, at the top, a heavy door opening into a tower room. Inside, there was a little old man with a bristle of untidy hair. Sir Brian sprang in and seized him by the neck.

'Ha, foul wizard,' shouted Sir Brian, 'I have thee!'

The old man at once turned into a lion. Sir Brian held fast. The lion became a fanged wolf. Sir Brian with a laugh still held him. The wolf became a dragon. Sir Brian held on. The dragon, in the blink of an eye, turned into a lady.

'Oh, you're hurting me,' said the lady.

'Not very knightly of you.'

'I beg your pardon,' said Sir Brian. He let go at once. The enchanter promptly waved his hand and turned Sir Brian into a pelican, which gave a dismal squawk and flew out of the window.

The enchanter changed back into himself and began to dust off his cloak. At that instant, Sir Philbert, who had seen the whole thing from the doorway, rushed in and grabbed the enchanter by the neck.

'What? Another one?' shrieked the enchanter.

He was so confused that he turned himself into a dreadful combination of lion, wolf, dragon, and woman all at once. Sir Philbert gritted his teeth and hung on. The enchanter then turned into a unicorn, a falcon, a salmon, a chest of drawers, a sabre-toothed tiger, and a burning waste-paper basket. Sir Philbert held on for dear life. At last, the enchanter turned into a wasp. This time, Sir Philbert almost did let go. But he thought of his health and of Victoria and of poor blustering Sir Brian, who was now a pelican, and he gripped the wasp tightly. It didn't sting him after all. Instead, it turned back into the enchanter, looking extremely sulky.

'Very well,' he panted. 'You've won.

What is your wish?'

'I want you to take the spell off Sir Brian,' said Sir Philbert.

'What, right now?'

'At once.'

The enchanter chuckled disagreeably. 'Very well,' he said. He waved his hand. Sir Brian, who was at that moment flying over a swamp, changed back into himself and fell *plop*! into the mud.

'Anything else?' said the enchanter.

'Yes,' said Sir Philbert, remembering the reason for the quest. 'I want you to let the Emperor's daughter go.'

'Let her go? How can I let her go when I haven't got her?'

'Oh, my,' groaned Sir Philbert. 'I knew it was the wrong castle. Well, who did kidnap her?'

'She was kidnapped by Brasilgore,' said the enchanter. 'And she has already been rescued.'

'She has? Where is she?'

'Downstairs in my courtyard,' snarled the enchanter. 'Now, if there's nothing else I can do for you, will you please go away?'

But Sir Philbert had already gone, down the stairs two at a time.

'And so Brasilgore the enchanter was

the giant,' he said as he and Victoria went trotting off together, she riding more comfortably on Sir Brian's horse. 'But why didn't you tell us?'

'You never asked me,' Victoria replied.

'That's true. Well, I suppose I'd better take you home to your father as quickly as possible.'

They travelled until they came to the Emperor's Empire. They entered the great city, and all the people ran out to

cheer and stare and point. They came to the castle, and there was the Emperor on a throne of ivory and emeralds. There also was Sir Brian, looking very muddy and rusty and bothered.

'Victoria, my darling, I'm so glad to see

you again,' said the Emperor, embracing her. 'Sir Brian was telling me how he had failed to find you.'

Victoria hugged her father. 'I must just tell you everything that has happened,' she cried. And so she did.

When she was finished, the Emperor said, 'I have sworn to give half my kingdom and my daughter's hand to the man brave enough to rescue her.'

Sir Philbert blushed. 'My lord,' he said, 'I really don't want half your kingdom. I have a nice little castle of my own, and it's all I can do to manage it — but I *would* rather like to have Victoria.'

Victoria smiled and took his hand.

Then Sir Brian interrupted. 'My lord Emperor,' he cried, 'that man didn't rescue your daughter by bravery. He killed the giant by accident and the cockatrice by a trick.'

'Dear me,' said the Emperor. He stroked his beard thoughtfully. 'Now let me get this straight. Where is Sir Hugo of Brandish?'

'He died a hero's death, sire,' said Sir Brian.

'I see. And Sir Armet of Anguish?'

'Perished bravely in combat.'

'Ah. And as for you, you'd still be a

pelican if it hadn't been for Sir Philbert, eh?'

Sir Brian frowned. 'But he is a coward!' he said.

'Ah, yes, there's that.' The Emperor turned to one of his servants and whispered in his ear. The servant turned pale and ran off. He came back in a few moments with a large box. From the box came a loud and angry humming.

'Now, gallant sirs,' said the Emperor, 'here is a box containing a wasps' nest. I'd like one of you to reach inside and catch a wasp for me. There is no reward. I just want a wasp.'

Sir Brian reached out a hand, listened to the furious humming, winced, and drew it back. Nobody else moved.

'You see,' said the Emperor. 'When Sir Philbert held on to the enchanter he was being quite as brave as was necessary. Sir Philbert, will you reach in and get me a wasp?'

Sir Philbert swallowed hard. He had had more practice than anyone, so to speak, but he didn't much want to do it again. Then, suddenly he had an idea. He grinned. He pulled on one of his iron gloves, reached into the box, and took out a wasp.

Victoria laughed. She said to her father, 'He's the only one of him there is, and I'm the only one of me there is, and he knows how to take care of both of us.'

'Quite right,' said the Emperor. 'I'd much rather have my daughter married to someone with sense enough to stay alive and take care of her than have her married to a pelican.'

So Philbert and Victoria were married and rode happily home to take care of each other.

The Dribblesome Teapots

Norman Hunter

Tea was more than just an ordinary afternoon sort of affair in Sypso-Sweetleigh. It was positively a State function, yes it was. The King and Queen would as soon have thought of missing their own coronation as missing their tea.

There were eight kinds of bread and butter and sixteen kinds of cake, ranging from the very plain and wholesome to the terribly indigestible and delicious. The tea-service was of gold except the teapot, and that was a lovely big brown earthenware one, known as a Brown Betty. The

Queen declared it was the only kind of pot
that made good tea. It had the royal
arms on the inside as well as the outside because the Queen was so specially
thorough she couldn't bear to think that
things you didn't see weren't as nice as
those you did. She always washed her
neck much farther down than necessary;
she insisted on all the cupboards being
tidy inside and she even had her shoes
polished on the soles, which was rather
awkward sometimes because they made
her slither about on the carpet. Still, she
had learned to skate ages ago, so she
managed to slither majestically.

'I declare I'm simply gasping for a cup
of tea,' said Her Majesty one day when it
was getting half-past-fourish.

'My dear, ought you to gasp?' asked
the King. He was known as King

Nutherkupp I I because that sounded nice and royal, but his real name was Leslie Jones. 'I mean to say,' he added, 'it isn't very majestic, is it?'

'It may not be very majestic,' said the Queen, 'but it is most exceedingly very true,' and she rang the bell for tea so hard that all the servants came hurrying in at once.

'Now, now, now,' said the Queen, 'I didn't ring for all of you. You know perfectly well I ring once for the butler, twice for the footman, three times for the parlour-maids, four times for the cook and so on.'

'Pardon, Majesty,' said the butler, bowing so low that a clump of picture cards he was collecting from tea-packets fell out of his waistcoat pocket all over the floor and were picked up by the first and second footmen who were collecting the same set. 'Your Majesty rang so many times we were not quite sure if you were ringing once a lot of times, or twice not so many times, or three times several times, or . . .'

'Oh, go away, all of you,' cried the Queen, shooing them out like a lot of chickens. 'I rang for tea, and please hurry up with it.' She sat down and went on gasping to herself, while the King tried to make up his mind whether to have plain wholesome cake which was good for him, but which he didn't like, or delicious creamy pastries which he loved, but which gave him pains.

Then in came tea with the butler all of a tremble, but trying not to show it because, most terrible of things to occur, he had chipped a bit off the spout of the Queen's Brown Betty!

'Perhaps Her Majesty won't notice it,' he thought. 'It's only a weeny little chip.' So he had rubbed a chocolate éclair on the chipped part to make it dark like the rest of the teapot and was hoping for the best and wondering how he could prepare for the worst, not knowing what the worst might be.

'Ah, tea at last,' said the Queen, brightening up, while the King suddenly made up his mind to have some of the plain wholesome cake first while he was hungry and then go on to the creamy pastries afterwards and hope that the plain wholesome cake would stop the pains that the creamy pastries gave him from being very noticeable.

The Queen began to pour out. And goodness gracious, how awful! The chipped spout of the Brown Betty made

the tea dribble all over the tablecloth and all over her robes!

For a moment there was silence except for the drip, drip, drip of the tea on to the carpet. The butler came over so queer that the footman gave him back the tea-packet cards, but still he felt no better.

'O-o-o-o-oh, disgraceful,' screamed the Queen, jumping up and putting the tea-pot down with such a bang that three lumps of sugar jumped out of the bowl into the King's tea; which he didn't at all mind because the Queen would never give him enough sugar anyway.

'Look at my lovely robes,' moaned the Queen, 'and oh, look at my lovely table-cloth, the one that Aunt Chrissie made for me with her own hands too! Not that she could have made it with anybody else's hands, but oh dear me, I shall cry, I know I shall.'

But she didn't cry, she went on talking and wailing and moaning and wringing her hands while the footmen began wringing the tablecloth to get the dribbled-over tea out of it. But alas and alack, they wrung it over the King's cake and made it all squodgy so that he had to have creamy pastries after all, pains or no pains, though it was pains all right as it turned out. Not that it was all right, him having pains, you know, but neither was it the least bit all right the Queen's teapot going all dribbly like that.

'If there's one thing I cannot stand, it's a teapot that dribbles,' cried the Queen. 'Oh, and that one was such a beautiful pourer. I can't understand what can have happened.'

The butler could understand perfectly well, but he simply dared not tell the

Queen about chipping the spout. So he said, 'I will fetch another teapot, Majesty.'

He fetched the best silver pot that was never used. But that was so ancient, having been part of the crown jewels of Sypso-Sweetleigh or something for years and years, that it was full of holes and dribbled in all directions instead of only at the spout.

'Oh, get me a teapot that doesn't dribble!' cried the Queen, gasping more than ever for her tea and not caring whether it was majestic or otherwise.

'Er-er-yes, Majesty,' said the butler.

He brought the kitchen teapot, which was enamel and always had dribbled, only the cook always held a bit of sponge under it. He brought a toy teapot from the little princess's toy cupboard, but that had no spout, and he brought two little ornamental sort of teapots with 'A present from Brighton' written on them and which didn't dribble because they were solid right through so weren't any more use than if they had.

'Oh, oh, oh, oh! this is terrible,' cried the Queen. 'Not a teapot in the palace that can be used. Oh, disgraceful! I must have a teapot that doesn't dribble, I must, I

must. Half the kingdom reward for anyone who can bring me a teapot that pours
without dribbling!'

'Here, here, here, half a mo!' cried the
King, getting all flurried and agitated and
forgetting to speak regally. 'You can't do
that. What do you think's going to
happen to Sypso-Sweetleigh if you go
offering half of it for teapots?'

But it was too late. The royal herald
who was a fearfully anxious-to-please sort
of person had dashed out the minute the
Queen said 'half the kingdom for a teapot
that pours without dribbling', and before
he could be caught and told to stop he had
shouted the proclamation all round the
city.

'Oh dear, oh dear, now you have done it,
you have,' cried the King. 'Half the kingdom for a teapot! Oh, it's awful! As if you
couldn't have gone up the road and
bought another teapot. Those proclamation and reward sort of businesses are
only meant for getting the kingdom saved
from dragons and things like that. I do
wish you'd be more careful.'

But the Queen wasn't listening. She'd
gone away to change her robes while the
cook poured her out a cup of tea in the
garden where the dribbles didn't matter

and brought it in to her with the saucer over the cup.

The butler, in despair at having caused such a to-do and a commotion, went straight to the court magician for advice, and hadn't been there more than two minutes when the King came in too, so he had to go out again without knowing whether the magician could do anything about anything or not.

'This is terrible,' said the King; 'the Queen has offered half the kingdom for a teapot that pours without dribbling and the proclamation is all over the town. What can we do? Can't you unproclamate it or something?'

'Alas, no, Majesty,' said the court magician, offering the King a pack of cards and asking him to take one and not say which one it was. But the King couldn't be bothered with conjuring sort of things, so smacked the cards up into the air in a shower where they all turned into birds and flew out of the window, except the one that the magician was going to make the King take, and that became a piece of gingerbread which the magician swallowed at one go while smoke came out of his ears.

'Well, well, you must do something

about it, you know,' said the King. 'What's the use of a court magician if he can't do an impossibility or so now and again for the good of the country?'

'Well,' said the magician, 'these things have to be thought out very carefully, you know, and sometimes one can get round a thing one can't do by doing several things one can do. For instance, supposing Your Majesty had been magicked and had three heads and came to me to make you have one head again; well, I couldn't do it, but what I could do would be to turn you into a newspaper, and then back into a king with only one head.'

'I see,' said the King, who didn't see at all really and began to think magic was a bit over-rated.

'Depend upon me, Majesty,' said the magician, producing a cup of cocoa from his hat and beginning to sip it. 'I will find a way to save the kingdom.'

So the King had to be satisfied with that, and the magician sat up all night reading the most unlikely books and practising unheard-of incantations.

The next morning the grounds of the palace were packed with people. It was like Lord Mayor's Show Day and Boat

Race Day and Cup Final and Coronation Day and Royal Garden Party and Opening of Parliament all at once. Everybody in the kingdom seemed to be there. And everybody had brought at least one teapot; most of them had brought several and one or two of them had brought simply cartloads of teapots. There were teapots of every size, shape and colour. Enormous teapots for the most extensive tea-parties and tiny little personal teapots for tea in bed. Some of the teapots didn't even look like teapots and one that did look most extravagantly like a teapot wasn't a teapot at all, but a tremendous imitation one as big as a bath that used to hang outside the chief tea shop.

'There now,' exclaimed the King, 'now do you see what you've done with your offer of half the kingdom for a teapot? Look at them! All with teapots. And unless I'm greatly mistaken practically every one of those teapots will pour without dribbling and how we're going to give away absolutely hundreds of halves of kingdoms and what we're going to do with absolutely hundreds of teapots with none of the kingdom left to put them in I do not know. It's terrible!'

'Oh, but can't we say we've changed our

minds,' said the Queen, 'and give them all a bag of oranges and send them home?'

'Bag of oranges!' snorted the King. 'And do you suppose that people who have come here with teapots hoping to get half the kingdom will go home quietly with bags of oranges? Why, there'd be a revolution or something. Not that it makes much difference,' he added gloomily. 'Something dreadful will come of this anyway. I don't see how it can help itself.'

His Majesty went downstairs and consulted with the prime minister.

'There's only one thing to do, Majesty,' said the prime minister. 'We must let them all bring their teapots in and make tea in them and see if they pour without dribbling.'

'Yes, and suppose they all pour without dribbling?' asked the King, throwing out his hands and hunching up his shoulders and raising his eyebrows all at once.

The prime minister didn't get a chance to answer that, for just then in swept the Queen.

'Now then,' she said firmly. 'I'm going to find a teapot that doesn't dribble whatever else happens. Tell them to bring in their teapots.'

So the people began to come in with their teapots. The first pot was handed to the King, who gave it to the butler, who made tea in it and handed it to the Queen, who poured out from it.

It dribbled all over the place!

More tea was made in the second pot and that dribbled worse than the first.

And the third and fourth and fifth and sixth and goodness knows how many tea-pots had tea made in them and tea poured from them, and goodness gracious, would you believe it, they all dribbled. Yes, they did, every single one of them. Some of the big pots dribbled more than some of the little pots and some of the little pots dribbled more than the big ones. Some of them dribbled to the left and some to the right and some all ways at once.

'Thank goodness!' exclaimed the King to himself. 'Oh, if only they all dribble we're saved.'

By this time the pots were being filled with tea and poured out a dozen or so at a time, the footmen and parlour-maids help-ing the Queen, and holding three pots in each hand. The prime minister took off his shoes and stockings to save them getting wet. Everywhere was getting as squishy as squishy.

'Oh dear, oh dear, this is awful,' sobbed the Queen. 'Oh, shan't I ever get a teapot that doesn't dribble?'

At last, every single teapot had been tried and every single one dribbled most horribly. The people went home all disappointed and puzzled and made themselves tea at home and found that their teapots poured out quite all right without dribbling. It was most mysterious.

'Well,' said the King, as the last person left the palace, 'that saves the kingdom anyway, though I must say it seems to have ruined the carpet.'

'But my teapot, oh, my teapot,' wailed the Queen. 'Oh, I'd do anything to have a teapot that pours without dribbling.'

'Your Majesty,' said a voice.

They all turned. It was the magician.

'Listen,' he said in his most magishy voice. 'The reason Your Majesty's Brown Betty dribbled was because the butler quite accidentally chipped a weeny bit off the spout.'

'Oh!' gasped the Queen. 'Off with his head,' she shouted, but the King very hurriedly said, 'No no, shush, please wait a minute,' only just in time to prevent the herald rushing off for the executioner.

'I couldn't magic the proclamation

away once it had been proclamated. There are some things even a magician can't do, and that is one of them,' went on the magician. 'So in order to save the kingdom from being given away in halves all over the place, I laid a spell on all the teapots in the kingdom to make them dribble.'

'Oh!' said the Queen again, and she was just going to cry 'Off with his head' when she remembered it wasn't much good offing with a magician's head because he'd have just put it back again.

'Now, Your Majesty,' continued the magician, 'I'm sure you will realize that the butler didn't mean to chip the Brown Betty teapot, and if you promise not to do anything nasty to him I will just do a small magic and mend the Brown Betty so that it will pour without dripping.'

'Yes, yes, I promise,' said the Queen eagerly.

So the Brown Betty was brought in and the magician did his small magic. Then tea was made in the Brown Betty.

'I bet it dribbles,' said the prime minister, who had begun to believe that all teapots would always dribble for evermore, he'd seen so many of them doing it.

The Queen picked up the Brown Betty and poured out a cup of tea.

The teapot didn't dribble so much as a spot!

She poured out cup after cup and not one dribble did the Brown Betty drib.

'Thank goodness for that,' exclaimed the King, and he went out for a nice game of croquet to calm himself down, while the Queen, who thought it rather a shame after all to have disappointed everybody about half the kingdom, had a coloured picture of herself and the King sent to everyone who had brought a teapot. And some of them hung their picture in the dining-room and some in the bedroom. Some hung it upside down because they weren't sure which way it ought to go. (If *you* look at the picture upside down, you will see why they weren't sure.) And some kept it to frighten their children with when they were naughty, which wasn't very polite to the King and Queen, but then perhaps it wasn't a very good picture.

Hare Takes Mr Knowall Badger Down a Peg or Two

Elizabeth Robinson

In his grassy nest in Bramble Patch Hare stretched and looked at his watch. 'Time to get up, Hare old fellow!' he told himself.

Hare had found the watch on Clover Hill. It had no hands, so it didn't tell the time; but to pretend that it did made Hare feel important. And more than anything else, Hare liked to feel important.

Hare was the postman. He wore a

postman's peaked cap, and carried a postman's bag. Written on the bag in large
blue letters were the words:

HARE ESQUIRE, POSTMAN AND
MESSENGER.

This made Hare feel important, too.

Although he went each day to look in
the hollow tree which served as the letter
box, Hare seldom found a letter in it; but
Badger usually had some message or
other for him to deliver, or some errand to
run. Badger was very fond of telling other
folk what to do.

On this particular morning Hare settled
his postman's peaked cap carefully
between his long, upstanding ears, and
slung his mail bag over his shoulder. Then
he left his nest — with two flying leaps to
foil any enemy that might try to follow his
scent there — and went lollopy-gallopy,
lollopy-gallopy, along the Pathway by
Rippling Stream, where he stopped to
breakfast on the juicy bark of a young
willow tree.

There was a flash of blue, and Kingfisher came to perch on a willow branch
close to Hare's nose.

'Good morning, Hare,' he said.

'Good morning, Kingfisher,' Hare

replied. 'Is there any news this morning?'
For little escaped Kingfisher's sharp eyes
as he sped swiftly hither and thither. He
heard all the news, and passed it on.

'Well . . .' began Kingfisher. Then, spot-
ting a fish in Rippling Stream, he dived
like a streak of blue ribbon and returned
to his perch with the fish in his beak.

'Well . . . what?' prompted Hare
impatiently.

Kingfisher tossed the fish in the air, and
caught it again, and swallowed it down
headfirst. 'Well . . .' he said once more, in
a just-swallowed-a-whole-fish sort of
voice, 'they do say that Owl's Oak is to
come down. And Hedgehog is awake at
last.'

'Owl's Oak to come down! *That's* bad
news,' said Hare. 'But I'm pleased to hear
that Hedgehog is awake. I've missed him.
Why he wants to sleep the winter away
beats me.'

'Me, too,' agreed Kingfisher. 'It's time
he woke up, the paths are a disgrace.' For
Hedgehog was the pathsweeper. With a
handcart and besom he cleaned up the
rubbish which careless picnickers left
behind.

Having finished his own breakfast,
Hare left Kingfisher to finish his, and

hurried on, lollopy-gallopy, to the Wild-wood, where he pushed his way through the undergrowth until he came to the gaping entrance to Badger's set.

Tripping clumsily over a pile of dry leaves and bracken, Hare tumbled head-long into Badger's fusty, dusty living-room.

Badger was snoozing in a fat, over-stuffed armchair by the fireplace. He rose in alarm. 'Oh, it's you, Hare,' he said dis-approvingly. 'You clumsy creature. You startled me.'

'Sorry, Badger. Very sorry indeed,' Hare apologised. It didn't do to upset Badger. In extreme circumstances he had been known to turn even on his friends, and make a meal of them. 'I tripped over that pile of old rubbish in your doorway,' Hare explained.

'Rubbish?' growled Badger. 'That isn't rubbish, Hare. That is my winter bedding

put out to air. It is springtime, Hare. Or hadn't you noticed?'

'I know it is springtime,' said Hare. 'Hedgehog is awake. And guess what, Badger? Owl's Oak is to come down!'

But Badger wasn't interested today in any news which Hare might have brought. 'I have been waiting for you, Hare,' he said. 'I want you to run to Mrs Mole's shop and buy some screws for me.'

'Screws!' exclaimed Hare. 'What do you want with screws, Badger?'

'I am going to build a bookcase,' Badger replied proudly. 'For my book.'

'A bookcase — for one book!' scoffed Hare. 'It will have to be a very small bookcase.'

'I shall one day acquire more books,' said Badger loftily. 'Education is a fine thing, Hare. A very fine thing.'

Badger had on his mantelpiece a big, black clock, which had a space under it. Badger kept all kinds of things in the space under this clock. He took from it now a piece of paper. 'Here is a list of the screws which I need,' he told Hare.

As he sped off through the Wildwood once more, Hare thought that Badger had never been quite the same since he had found that book about water-bugs, left behind near Rippling Stream by some picnicker. He had always fancied himself, but now he was quite impossible, with all his talk of education. He even kept some prize water-bugs in a bucket in his kitchen. Mistaking the water-bug bucket for the water bucket one day, Hare had almost swallowed some of them. Almost swallowing some of Badger's prize water-bugs had given Hare a very nasty shock.

Mrs Mole's shop was tucked away in the bracken in a corner of the Wildwood. It had white bow windows on either side of a white door. Hare had to stoop to enter it. Mrs Mole, wearing a frilled cap and apron, stood behind the counter. She peered short-sightedly up at Hare.

'Good morning, Hare,' she said. 'What can I get for you today?'

'Good morning, Mrs Mole,' Hare replied. 'I would like some screws, please. For Badger. Badger is going to build a bookcase,' he added proudly. Hare might scoff at Badger; nevertheless, he felt a little proud to have a friend who was going to build a bookcase.

'Fancy that, now!' exclaimed Mrs Mole, much impressed. 'I'm afraid I have no screws at present, Hare. I'm not often asked for them. But no doubt Mole will be

able to find some for me, when he goes to the town. It's surprising what Mole manages to find by scrabbling about in the town.'

'Really?' said Hare. He had no idea what a town was; but he had no intention of showing his ignorance by asking Mrs Mole to tell him. He wished her a polite good-day and went thoughtfully on his way.

On turning a corner who should Hare see but Hedgehog, with his handcart by his side, and busily at work with his besom.

'Good morning, Hedgehog,' said Hare. 'Have you had a good sleep this winter?'

Hedgehog stopped brushing the path with his besom, and leant on it instead. 'I have had a very good sleep, thank you, Hare,' he said. 'Has anything interesting happened while I've been sleeping?'

'Badger found a book about water-bugs by Rippling Stream, and he has decided to build a bookcase to put it in,' replied Hare.

'A book, eh! *And* a bookcase. Badger is going up in the world,' said Hedgehog, clearly much impressed. 'When shall we see this bookcase, Hare?'

'He can't begin to build it until Mrs Mole gets some screws,' Hare explained. 'She is going to ask Mole to bring some back from the town.'

'Oh, yes,' said Hedgehog solemnly. Hedgehog didn't know what a town was either; but he had no intention of showing his ignorance by asking Hare to tell him. The two of them stood looking at each other, each wondering whether the other knew what a town was, but neither willing to show his ignorance by asking the other.

'From *the town*, you said?' Hedgehog remarked thoughtfully at last.

'That's right,' said Hare. 'Mrs Mole says it's surprising what Mole manages to find by scrabbling about in *the town*.'

'Is that so?' said Hedgehog, staring with bright little eyes at Hare. Hare decided he had better be on his way before Hedgehog asked him a question about a town, which he wouldn't be able to answer. He looked at his watch. 'Goodness!' he exclaimed. 'Is that the time? I must dash.'

'What *is* the time, Hare?' Hedgehog asked mischievously.

'Late,' replied Hare. 'Very late, Hedgehog. Goodbye.'

Somehow, thought Hare as he sped lollopy-gallopy to Badger's set, I must find out from Badger what a town is — without actually asking him, of course. For there is nothing more damaging to one's sense of importance than not knowing what something is.

'You have taken your time, Hare,' Badger grumbled. 'Have you got the screws for me?'

'No, Badger,' Hare replied. 'Mrs Mole didn't have any screws. But she said she would ask Mole to bring some back from *the town*.'

'Oh, yes,' said Badger solemnly.

'Mrs Mole says it is surprising what Mole manages to find by scrabbling about in *the town*,' said Hare.

'Oh, yes,' said Badger once more. And something in his manner, and the way he said, 'Oh, yes,' told Hare that for all his fine talk about education, Badger didn't know what a town was either.

If I can find out what a town is, I shall know something which Badger doesn't know, thought Hare. He thought how important he would feel if he were able to tell Badger something he didn't know.

Quickly Hare took his leave of Badger and returned to his grassy nest in Bramble Patch to have a good think.

Somehow, he decided, he had to find out what a town was; and it was important that whoever he learned it from shouldn't guess that he didn't know, because they might tell Badger.

It wouldn't be easy, but Hare was a cunning fellow. And the very next morning he had a piece of luck in the matter. As he went along the Pathway he came upon Kingfisher, sitting in his favourite willow by Rippling Stream, hiccoughing gently as he regurgitated the bones of his fishy breakfast.

Hare, a vegetarian himself, usually found this spectacle displeasing; but today he was prepared to put up with it.

'Good morning, Kingfisher,' he said. 'Is there any news today?'

'Yes,' replied Kingfisher. 'Badger is going to build a bookcase for the book which he found underneath this very willow tree.'

'I know,' said Hare. 'But who told you about it, Kingfisher?'

'Badger told me himself,' replied Kingfisher. 'He stopped by on his way home from his night's hunting. He told me about the bookcase. Then for some reason he began to talk about towns, and how some folk didn't know what a town was. Of course, I said that only someone who was very stupid indeed wouldn't know what a town was. And Badger went off in a huff! Do you know what I think, Hare? I think that for all his fine talk about education, Badger doesn't know what a town is! He probably thinks there is nothing else in all the world but the Wildwood, Bramble Patch, Clover Hill, Rippling Stream and Big River. Would you credit it, Hare!'

'I never would!' exclaimed Hare, not willing for one moment to admit that *he* had thought there was nothing else in all the world but the Wildwood, Bramble Patch, Clover Hill, Rippling Stream and Big River.

'What did you tell him, Kingfisher?' Hare asked craftily. 'Did you tell him what a town was?'

'No, I didn't, because he didn't ask me,' replied Kingfisher. 'Can you imagine

Badger admitting there is something he doesn't know?'

'Now that you mention it, no, I can't,' said Hare. Then — 'Have you seen any towns lately, Kingfisher?' he asked.

'Seen any towns lately! Of course I have, Hare. I don't spend all my time in one place, as the rest of you seem to do. Why, I see a town every time I fly over the holly hedge on the far side of the Wildwood. And I do that almost every day. In fact, I am going to do it right now.' With a harsh screech Kingfisher flew, like a streak of blue ribbon, fast and low away down Rippling Stream.

Hare grinned to himself. He was well pleased with his morning's work so far. Of course, he didn't know yet *what* a town was. But he knew *where* one was. And before the morning was over — as soon as he had been and looked over the holly hedge on the far side of the Wildwood, in fact — he would know *what* it was. Or he would eat his postman's peaked cap!

And then he would know something Badger didn't know.

Hare set off, whistling softly to himself and thinking how he was going to enjoy knowing something Badger didn't know. And how important he was going to feel when he had passed this information on to Badger.

Badger was a nocturnal animal, which means he went out at night, and preferred to spend the daylight hours at home. Hare was surprised, therefore, and a little put out when, on his way through the Wildwood, who should he see but Badger, deep in conversation with Hedgehog.

When he saw Hare, Badger looked embarrassed; but Hedgehog was his usual cheerful, slightly mischievous self.

'Badger and I have just been talking about towns,' Hedgehog told Hare. 'If you recall, Hare, you and I were discussing towns when we met yesterday.'

'Er — yes, I believe we were,' Hare agreed uneasily.

Hedgehog's small bright eyes twinkled

mischievously. 'And do you know what I think, Hare? I think that Badger doesn't know what a town is! Would you credit that?'

'No, I never would,' said Hare.

'Er — um — grumph — what nonsense!' mumbled Badger. 'I am not staying here to listen to such rubbish. I have important things to do . . .'

Hare realized that if Badger were to escape now, he would probably refuse to discuss the subject again until he had somehow managed to find out for himself what a town was. So if he, Hare, was going to be the one to tell him, he must do it now. And what better time than when Hedgehog was here as well, to witness his triumph when he took Mr Knowall Badger down a peg or two!

Hare had just one problem: he didn't know yet himself what a town was. But he did know where to find one, and he was a cunning fellow.

So — 'Wait a minute, Badger,' he said. 'Let us ask *Hedgehog* to tell us what a town is. *If he knows*, that is.'

Badger hesitated. Hedgehog shuffled his feet. Then he rolled into a ball, speared a toffee paper on his spines, and slowly unrolled himself. 'There are some very untidy folk about,' he said.

'Hedgehog!' said Hare sternly. 'Don't try to change the subject. Do you or do you not know what a town is?'

Hedgehog shuffled his feet again, and looked thoughtful. 'Well,' he said, 'now that I come to think about it, I do believe I had one for my breakfast this morning.'

'Had one for your breakfast!' said Hare scornfully. 'A town isn't something you can eat!' He didn't *think* a town was something you could eat.

'I thought as much,' said Badger. 'Hedgehog doesn't know what a town is. Well, I'm off. As I said, I have important things to do . . .'

'Not so fast, Badger,' said Hare. 'Why don't you tell us what a town is. *If you know*, that is.'

Badger um-ed, ah-ed, and grumph-ed. 'Well, now that I come to think about it, I believe I have one under my clock,' he said.

'A town under your clock!' said Hare scornfully. 'A town isn't something you can keep under a clock!' He didn't *think* a town was something you could keep under a clock.

Badger stared sulkily down at his feet. 'Very well,' he said. 'Seeing as how you seem to know so much about it, Hare, *you* tell us what a town is!'

Hare, of course, had no more idea than Badger and Hedgehog what a town was.

'Ahem — for various reasons, a town is a very difficult thing for me to describe,' he said. 'If I were to try to do so, I might give you quite the wrong impression. But if you will come with me, I will do better than tell you what a town is. I will show one to you. Follow me, Badger and Hedgehog.'

Badger and Hedgehog followed Hare for a very long time.

'How much further must we go?' asked Hedgehog wearily at last.

'Not much further,' replied Hare.

'You might have told us what a town is, and saved us all this trouble,' grumbled Badger. 'I have important things to do . . .'

They came to the holly hedge. Over the holly hedge was the town. Hare led the way through a gap in the hedge, and stopped and looked about him.

'Well?' said Hedgehog expectantly.

'Well?' said Badger impatiently.

'Well . . .' said Hare uncertainly.

The town was there at their feet, far below in the valley. But today it was hidden under a thick blanket of fog. The fog was made thicker by smoke which poured from the chimneys of the houses and factories in the town. Fog such as this never came to the high windy ridge of the Wildwood, nor to Bramble Patch, Clover Hill or Rippling Stream. A fine mist hovered sometimes over Big River. But that was nothing like this dirty, thick, grey fog.

'Well ...' said Hare once more. Kingfisher had said that there was a town over the holly hedge. And the only thing in sight was this thick, dirty, grey stuff. 'Well ...' he said again, pointing to the fog. 'There you are, Badger and Hedgehog. *That* is a town.'

The fog rose up and made their eyes smart.

'Pah! Nasty dirty thing,' growled Badger. 'If that is a town, then I'm glad I *haven't* got one under my clock.'

'And if that is a town, then I'm glad I *didn't* have one for breakfast,' said Hedgehog. 'But thank you all the same, Hare, for showing it to us,' he added politely.

'It has been my pleasure!' Hare assured him happily.

Then, grinning all over his face and feeling very important indeed, Hare led the way back through the Wildwood. For hadn't he just proved that he knew something Mr Knowall Badger hadn't known!

Send Three and Fourpence, We Are Going to a Dance

Jan Mark

Mike and Ruth Dixon got on well enough, but not so well that they wanted to walk home from school together. Ruth would not have minded, but Mike, who was two classes up, preferred to amble along with his friends so that he usually arrived a long while after Ruth did.

Ruth was leaning out of the kitchen window when he came in through the side gate, kicking a brick.

'I've got a message for you,' said Mike. 'From school. Miss Middleton wants you to go and see her tomorrow before assembly, and take a dead frog.'

'What's she want *me* to take a dead frog for?' said Ruth. 'She's not my teacher. I haven't got a dead frog.'

'How should I know?' Mike let himself in. 'Where's Mum?'

'Round Mrs Todd's. Did she really say a dead frog? I mean, really say it?'

'Derek told me to tell you. It's nothing to do with me.'

Ruth cried easily. She cried now. 'I bet she never. You're pulling my leg.'

'I'm not, and you'd better do it. She said it was important — Derek said — and you know what a rotten old temper she's got,' said Mike, feelingly.

'But why me? It's not fair.' Ruth leaned her head on the window-sill and wept in earnest. 'Where'm I going to find a dead frog?'

'Well, you can peel them off the road

74

sometimes when they've been run over. They go all dry and flat, like pressed flowers,' said Mike. He did think it a trifle unreasonable to demand dead frogs from little girls, but Miss Middleton *was* unreasonable. Everyone knew that. 'You could start a pressed frog collection,' he said.

Ruth sniffed fruitily. 'What do you think Miss'll do if I don't get one?'

'She'll go barmy, that's what,' said Mike. 'She's barmy anyway,' he said. 'Nah, don't start howling again. Look, I'll go down the ponds after tea. I know there's frogs there because I saw the spawn, back at Easter.'

'But those frogs are alive. She wants a dead one.'

'I dunno. Perhaps we could get it put to sleep or something, like Mrs Todd's Tibby was. And don't tell Mum. She doesn't like me down the ponds and she won't let us have frogs indoors. Get an old box with a lid and leave it on the rockery, and I'll put old Froggo in it when I come home. *And stop crying*!'

After Mike had gone out Ruth found the box that her summer sandals had come in. She poked air holes in the top and furnished it with damp grass and a tin lid full of water. Then she left it on the rockery with a length of darning wool so that Froggo could be fastened down safely until morning. It was only possible to imagine Froggo alive; all tender and green and saying croak-croak. She could not think of him dead and flat and handed over to Miss Middleton, who definitely must have gone barmy. Perhaps Mike or Derek had been wrong about the dead part. She hoped they had.

She was in the bathroom, getting ready for bed, when Mike came home. He looked round the door and stuck up his thumbs.

'Operation Frog successful. Over and out.'

'Wait. Is he . . . alive?'

'Shhh. Mum's in the hall. Yes.'

'What's he like?'

'Sort of frog-shaped. Look, I've got him; OK? I'm going down now.'

'Is he green?'

'No. More like that pork pie that went mouldy on top. Good night!'

Mike had hidden Froggo's dungeon under the front hedge, so all Ruth had to do next morning was scoop it up as she went out of the gate. Mike had left earlier with his friends, so she paused for a moment to introduce herself. She tapped quietly on the lid. 'Hullo?'

There was no answering cry of croak-croak. Perhaps he *was* dead. Ruth felt a tear coming and raised the lid a fraction at one end. There was a scrabbling noise and at the other end of the box she saw something small and alive, crouching in the grass.

'Poor Froggo,' she whispered through the air holes. 'I won't let her kill you, I promise,' and she continued on her way to school feeling brave and desperate, and ready to protect Froggo's life at the cost of her own.

The school hall was in the middle of the building and classrooms opened off it. Miss Middleton had Class 3 this year, next to the cloakroom. Ruth hung up her blazer, untied the wool from Froggo's box, and went to meet her doom. Miss Middleton was arranging little stones in an aquarium on top of the bookcase, and jerked her head when Ruth knocked, to show that she should come in.

'I got him, Miss,' said Ruth, holding out the shoe box in trembling hands.

'What, dear?' said Miss Middleton, up to her wrists in water-weed.

'Only he's not dead and I won't let you kill him!' Ruth cried, and swept off the lid with a dramatic flourish. Froggo, who must have been waiting for this, sprung out, towards Miss Middleton, landed with a clammy sound on that vulnerable place between the collar bones, and slithered down inside Miss Middleton's blouse.

Miss Middleton taught Nature Study. She was not afraid of little damp creatures, but she was not expecting Froggo. She gave a squawk of alarm and jumped backwards. The aquarium skidded in the opposite direction; took off; shattered against a desk. The contents broke over Ruth's new sandals in a tidal wave, and Lily the goldfish thrashed about in a shallow puddle on the floor. People came running with mops and dustpans. Lily Fish was taken out by the tail to recover in the cloakroom sink. Froggo was arrested while trying to leave Miss Middleton's blouse through the gap between two buttons, and put back in his box with a weight on top in case he made another dash for freedom.

Ruth, crying harder than she had ever done in her life, was sent to stand outside the headmaster's room, accused of playing stupid practical jokes; and cruelty to frogs.

Sir looked rather as if he had been laughing, but it seemed unlikely, under the circumstances, and Ruth's eyes were so swollen and tear-filled that she couldn't see clearly. He gave her a few minutes to dry out and then said,

'This isn't like you, Ruth. Whatever possessed you to go throwing frogs at poor Miss Middleton? And poor frog, come to that.'

'She told me to bring her a frog,' said Ruth, stanching another tear at the injustice of it all. 'Only she wanted a dead one, and I couldn't find a dead one, and I couldn't kill Froggo. I won't kill him,' she said, remembering her vow on the way to school.

'Miss Middleton says she did not ask you to bring her a frog, or kill her a frog. She thinks you've been very foolish and unkind,' said Sir, 'and I think you are not telling the truth. Now . . .'

'Mike told me to,' said Ruth.

'Your brother? Oh, come now.'

'He did. He said Miss Middleton wanted me to go to her before assembly with a dead frog and I did, only it wasn't dead and I won't!'

'Ruth! Don't grizzle. No one is going to murder your frog, but we must get this nonsense sorted out.' Sir opened his door and called to a passer-by, 'Tell Michael Dixon that I want to see him at once, in my office.'

Mike arrived, looking wary. He had heard the crash and kept out of the way, but a summons from Sir was not to be ignored.

'Come in, Michael,' said Sir. 'Now, why did you tell your sister that Miss Middleton wanted her to bring a dead frog to school?'

'It wasn't me,' said Mike. 'It was a message from Miss Middleton.'

'Miss Middleton told you?'

'No, Derek Bingham told me. She told him to tell me — I suppose,' said Mike, sulkily. He scowled at Ruth. All her fault.

'Then you'd better fetch Derek Bingham here right away. We're going to get to the bottom of this.'

Derek arrived. He too had heard the crash.

'Come in, Derek,' said Sir. 'I understand that you told Michael here some tarradiddle about his sister. You let him think it was a message from Miss Middleton, didn't you?'

'Yes, well . . .' Derek shuffled. 'Miss Middleton didn't tell *me*. She told, er, someone, and they told me.'

'Who was this someone?'

Derek turned all noble and stood up straight and pale. 'I can't remember, Sir.'

'Don't let's have any heroics about sneaking, Derek, or I shall get very *cross*.'

Derek's nobility ebbed rapidly. 'It was Tim Hancock, Sir. He said Miss Middleton wanted Ruth Dixon to bring her a dead dog before assembly.'

'A dead *dog*?'

'Yes, Sir.'

'Didn't you think it a bit strange that Miss Middleton should ask Ruth for a dead dog, Derek?'

'I thought she must have one, Sir.'

'But why should Miss Middleton want it?'

'Well, she does do Nature Study,' said Derek.

'Go and fetch Tim,' said Sir.

Tim had been playing football on the field when the aquarium went down. He

came in with an innocent smile which wilted when he saw what was waiting for him.

'Sir?'

'Would you mind repeating the message that you gave Derek yesterday afternoon?'

'I told him Miss Middleton wanted Sue Nixon to bring her a red sock before assembly,' said Tim. 'It was important.'

'Red sock? Sue Nixon?' said Sir. He was beginning to look slightly wild-eyed. 'Who's Sue Nixon? There's no one in this school called Sue Nixon.'

'I don't know any of the girls, Sir,' said Tim.

'Didn't you think a red sock was an odd

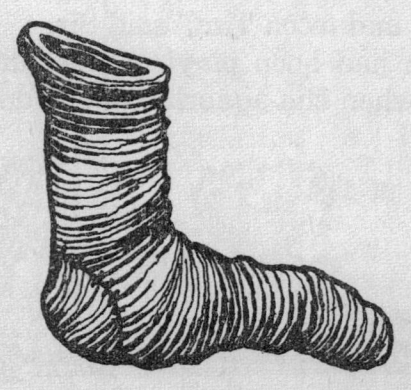

thing to ask for?'

'I thought she was bats, Sir.'

'Sue Nixon?'

'No, Sir. Miss Middleton, Sir,' said truthful Tim.

Sir raised his eyebrows. 'But why did you tell Derek?'

'I couldn't find anyone else, Sir. It was late.'

'But why Derek?'

'I had to tell someone or I'd have got into trouble,' said Tim, virtuously.

'You are in trouble,' said Sir. 'Michael, ask Miss Middleton to step in here for a moment, please.'

Miss Middleton, frog-ridden, looked round the door.

'I'm sorry to bother you again,' said Sir, 'but it seems that Tim thinks you told him that one Sue Nixon was to bring you a red sock before assembly.'

'Tim!' said Miss Middleton, very shocked. 'That's a naughty fib. I never told you any such thing.'

'Oh Sir,' said Tim, 'Miss didn't tell me. It was Pauline Bates done that.'

'*Did* that. I think I see Pauline out in the hall,' said Sir. 'In the PT class. Yes? Let's have her in.'

Pauline was very small and very frightened. Sir sat her on his knee and told her not to worry. 'All we want to know,' he said, 'is what you said to Tim yesterday. About Sue Nixon and the dead dog.'

'Red sock, Sir,' said Tim.

'Sorry. Red sock. Well, Pauline?'

Pauline looked as if she might join Ruth in tears. Ruth had just realized that she was no longer involved, and was crying with relief.

'You said Miss Middleton gave you a message for Sue Nixon. What was it?'

'It wasn't Sue Nixon,' said Pauline, damply. 'It was June Nichols. It wasn't Miss Middleton, it was Miss Wimbledon.'

'There *is* no Miss Wimbledon,' said Sir. 'June Nichols, yes. I know June, but Miss Wimbledon . . .?'

'She means Miss Wimpole, Sir,' said Tim. 'The big girls call her Wimbledon 'cause she plays tennis, Sir, in a little skirt.'

'I thought you didn't know any girls,' said Sir. 'What did Miss Wimpole say to you, Pauline?'

'She didn't,' said Pauline. 'It was Moira Thatcher. She said to tell June Nichols to come and see Miss Whatsit before assembly and bring her bed socks.'

'Then why tell Tim?'

'I couldn't find June. June's in his class.'

'I begin to see daylight,' said Sir. 'Not much, but it's there. All right, Pauline. Go and get Moira, please.'

Moira had recently had a new brace fitted across her front teeth. It caught the light when she opened her mouth.

'Yeth, Thir?'

'Moira, take it slowly, and tell us what the message was about June Nichols.'

Moira took a deep breath and polished the brace with her tongue.

'Well, Thir, Mith Wimpole thaid to thell June to thee her before athembly with her wed fw—thw—thth—'

'Frock?' said Sir. Moira nodded gratefully. 'So why tell Pauline?'

'Pauline liveth up her thtweet, Thir.'

'No I don't,' said Pauline. 'They moved. They got a council house, up the Ridgeway.'

'All right, Moira,' said Sir. 'Just ask Miss Wimpole if she could thp — spare me a minute of her time, please?'

If Miss Wimpole was surprised to find eight people in Sir's office, she didn't show it. As there was no longer room to get inside, she stood at the doorway and waved. Sir waved back. Mike instantly decided that Sir fancied Miss Wimpole.

'Miss Wimpole, I believe you must be the last link in the chain. Am I right in thinking that you wanted June Nichols to see you before assembly, with her red frock?'

'Why, yes,' said Miss Wimpole. 'She's dancing a solo at the end-of-term concert. I wanted her to practise, but she didn't turn up.'

'Thank you,' said Sir. 'One day, when we both have a spare hour or two, I'll tell you why she didn't turn up. As for you lot,' he said, turning to the mob round his desk, 'you seem to have been playing Chinese Whispers without knowing it. You also seem to think that the entire staff is off its head. You may be right. I don't know. Red socks, dead dogs, live frogs — we'll put your friend in the school pond, Ruth. Fetch him at break. And now, someone had better find June Nichols and deliver Miss Wimpole's message.'

'Oh, there's no point, Sir. She couldn't have come anyway,' said Ruth. 'She's got chicken-pox. She hasn't been at school for ages.'

Micawber

Ray Harris

War broke out in our new place the night we arrived. The trouble was Bully Beef, the cat next door. Apparently he had always looked on the back yard of the house we'd just bought, in the same way that a bunch of Chicago gangsters regard certain parts of Chicago — as his territory.

Our two tomcats, newly freed from their box, stalked round the yard, sniffed its nine gum-trees and took possession of it in the name of themselves. Then they whipped up on the fence and looked down into Bully Beef's yard, probably thinking that they might as well annex that too. But their first sight of Bully Beef removed that idea. The fellow certainly was a tough tomcat — and a mighty big one — and they could see murder in his slitted eyes. They jumped down into the long grass, then came up and sat together on the bottom step of the back porch, apprehension in every whisker.

The whole trouble with our chaps, of course, was that they'd got used to soft living and now they were practically sissies. Sooty was undersized and very particular about his appearance, always sponging down his white waistcoat and sponging Micawber's for him as well. Moreover, he always stood up when anyone entered a room — a perfect little Lord Fauntleroy, you might say. Micawber, the other chap, was a tabby. He was polite too, but he was big and spongy and bone lazy, and so stupid that you had to push his head down hard on a piece of meat before he got the idea that it was there and that he had your permission to eat it; and, from packing himself politely out of the way under traymobiles, bookcases or chairs, he'd got so that he couldn't relax

unless he had a roof over his head, so to speak. He'd sit under the traymobile by the hour — just sit as if he were waiting for something to turn up; which, of course, was why we called him Micawber. In short, they were such a refined, helpless couple of cats that Bully Beef's mouth fell open and stayed open when he saw them.

He didn't waste time before starting to enjoy himself, though. At 9.45 that first night he ambushed Sooty in the rank grass behind the laundry and had him cut to pieces before we could get to him. Inside an hour Sooty couldn't put even one foot to the ground, and, without nursing, he'd certainly have been done for.

Micawber was puzzled by him. He stayed near him all night, telling him bedtime stories, I suppose, and thinking hard in between. He was still puzzled next morning. And for a chap who'd never had to think and had never wanted to think, that must have been a strain, all right.

Well, about the middle of the afternoon he must have thought a stroll would clear his brain. He snooped through and under the long grass, down the full length of the yard and across, and then started back. He was about halfway back when there was a swish and Bully Beef shot up out of his ambush.

It was a beautifully timed spring, and Micawber didn't know what hit him till he was on his back with Bully Beef astride him. All we could see was Bully Beef's tabby back as he started tearing our chap up. Next minute Micawber somehow got clear. He shot up the steps and right in amongst us. Bully stopped at the steps and looked up obliquely, the way gangsters look, and he made it plain that the murder was only postponed. Then he spat through his teeth and strolled down the middle of the concrete path.

Micawber oozed under the rails of a porch chair while we threw things at Bully Beef and missed him. Then Micawber climbed out and went in and looked at the unhappy Sooty on the cushion we'd fixed for him. When Micawber looked up it seemed to me that there was just a flicker of intelligence in his eye, as though the fat-headed old softy had got around at last to the idea that what had happened to Sooty was what had very nearly happened to himself. But then he sighed, as much as to say, well, perhaps something would turn up to improve the situation, and went and packed himself in under the traymobile. He didn't look puzzled any more, though; he just sat there as if he were waiting, as I said, for something to turn up.

He was still there at bedtime, looking like a soft, tabby ball; so, as it was a hot night, I left the back door open, switched off the lights and went to bed.

It was about half daylight when I heard a series of death squawks that told me plainly that Bully Beef was now committing the second half of his murder. I pelted down the hall in my bare feet and out of

the back door. The bellowing came from out of the grass jungle and I could see Bully Beef astride of his victim, tearing and slashing. This time he had Micawber pinned down hard by the throat, and he was carving him with his hind claws, tossing his fur away behind in little clouds that floated over the grass. Now and then Micawber would get enough breath to bawl for help, and then Bully's teeth choked him quiet again. I jumped the steps and snatched up a rake. The murderer was too interested to see me. In one more leap I was out into the wet grass and raised the rake high — but I kept it raised, my mouth open.

It wasn't Bully Beef doing the murdering. Bully was down under, bellowing for police protection. But he had only a whimper left by this time and Micawber let go of his throat and started to chew his hind legs. And then the old idiot saw me. He straightened at once and stepped back politely. Bully choked, gasped a couple of times, then rolled over and got to his feet. He wobbled and fell, got up again, wobbled on to the path and zigzagged along it till at last he staggered round the corner of the house.

When I looked down again at Micawber, he was packing himself comfortably into a nest roofed over with tall grass tufts. By the look of the nest he'd been in it quite a while.

In fact you'd almost think he'd spent the night there, waiting for something to turn up.

Why Anna Hung
Upside Down

Margaret Mahy

One day Anna, wearing her blue jeans, went out and climbed on to the first branch of the second tree to the right of the supermarket.

Then she hung by her knees.

She saw the world upside down. The grass was the sky and the sky was the grass. The supermarket poured people upwards into the green air.

An old man with a ridiculous hat came
by.

'Look at this girl,' he said to a thin
woman with fluffy slippers and curlers.
'She's upside down.'

'My goodness so she is!' the thin
woman cried. 'Why do you think that's
happened?'

'I don't know,' the man replied.
'Perhaps it's the weather, we've had some
funny weather lately and it may be affect-
ing the children.'

'Perhaps she's doing it for health
reasons,' said a sickly looking goat.
'Being upside down lets the blood into the
brain, and that perks you up no end.'

A lion and a school inspector going
home from the supermarket stopped to
look on curiously. The lion said nothing,

but the school inspector said: 'It's the parents' fault. Parents let their children do anything these days. Now this poor child's parents are most likely at home drinking tea and reading the paper and not looking after their girl. *They* don't care that she's gone all upside down out here.'

'Yes, that's right!' called the mother of twins. 'They don't care at all. Now if my twins were to go all upside down like that, I'd smack them with the hair brush. That'd bring them right way up again pretty quick I can tell you.'

At this point, a boy called Ron, oldest of five, climbed up into the tree too and hung beside Anna.

'Look at that, now there's two of them at it,' cried an excited voice, probably a hen. There were quite a few hens in the crowd.

'It's catching, it's catching,' shouted the thin woman in fluffy slippers and the crowd moved back several steps nervously.

'I don't want to go upside down,' whimpered a rich man. 'All my money would fall out of my pockets.'

'Neither you shall!' said his pretty secretary, hurrying him away and looking angrily at Anna and Ron as she went.

'It's the new craze,' said a folk-singing crocodile strumming on her guitar. Then she sang showing long rows of well-kept teeth:

> '*Upside down — upside down —*
> *The newest craze to hit the town . . .*'

But at this point a little girl called Sally wearing a track suit climbed into the tree and hung by her knees next to Ron.

'I still say it's the weather!' cried the man in the ridiculous hat.

'Now then,' said a policeman coming up. 'What's all this?'

'Look, look, the police have come,' twittered some excitable guinea pigs, and a small number of culprits and criminals slunk away to evade the eye of the law.

'These poor children, neglected by their parents, have gone all upside down,' said the school inspector in an important voice.

'But perhaps,' suggested a professor of philosophy going by with a meat pie in a paper bag, 'perhaps they are the right way up. Perhaps it is we who are upside down.'

This upset a lot of people. There was a resentful muttering and the sound of gritting teeth.

The policeman had to do something quickly. People and animals were all upset. He thought hard.

'Send for the fire brigade,' he commanded at last.

But the lion, who had been watching thoughtfully, said in a deep lion's voice, 'Ask them! Ask them why they are hanging upside down.'

The policeman came up to Anna. 'Now

then, young lady!' he said, 'Why are you upside down in that tree?'

'I learned to do this yesterday,' replied Anna, 'I just wanted to see if I could still do it today.'

'It's fun!' shouted Ron. 'You all look funny upside down.'

And Sally shouted: 'Upside down frowns turn into smiles.'

Then Anna put up her hands and swung down from the branch, and so did Ron and Sally.

'Why are you doing that?' asked the man in the ridiculous hat.

'Well, the bend of my knees is starting to hurt a bit,' Anna said. 'And not only that, it's dinner time and hanging upside down makes you hungry. Are you coming?' And then all three walked away, leaving the first branch of the second tree to the right of the supermarket absolutely empty.

Henry and Ribs

Beverly Cleary

Henry Huggins was in the third grade. His hair looked like a scrubbing brush and most of his grown-up front teeth were in. He lived with his mother and father in a square white house on Klickitat Street. Except for having his tonsils out when he was six and breaking his arm falling out of a cherry-tree when he was seven, nothing much happened to Henry.

I wish something exciting would happen, Henry often thought.

But nothing very interesting ever happened to Henry, at least not until one

Wednesday afternoon in March. Every Wednesday after school Henry rode downtown on the bus to go swimming at the YMCA. After he swam for an hour, he got on the bus again and rode home just in time for dinner. It was fun but not really exciting.

When Henry left the YMCA on this particular Wednesday, he stopped to watch a man tear down a circus poster. Then, with three nickels and one dime in his pocket, he went to the corner drugstore to buy a chocolate ice cream cone. He thought he would eat the ice cream cone, get on the bus, drop his dime in the slot, and ride home.

That is not what happened.

He bought the ice cream cone and paid for it with one of his nickels. On his way out of the drugstore he stopped to look at funny books. It was a free look, because he had only two nickels left.

He stood there licking his chocolate ice cream cone and reading one of the funny books when he heard a thump, thump, thump. Henry turned, and there behind him was a dog. The dog was scratching himself. He wasn't any special kind of dog. He was too small to be a big dog but, on the other hand, he was much too big to be a little dog. He wasn't a white dog, because parts of him were brown and other parts were black and in between there were yellowish patches. His ears stood up and his tail was long and thin.

The dog was hungry. When Henry licked, he licked. When Henry swallowed, he swallowed.

'Hello, you old dog,' Henry said. 'You can't have my ice cream cone.'

Swish, swish, swish, went the tail. 'Just one bite,' the dog's brown eyes seemed to say.

'Go away,' ordered Henry. He wasn't very firm about it. He patted the dog's head.

The tail wagged harder. Henry took one last lick. 'Oh, all right,' he said. 'If you're that hungry, you might as well have it.'

The ice cream cone disappeared in one gulp.

'Now go away,' Henry told the dog. 'I have to catch a bus for home.' He started for the door. The dog started, too.

'Go away, you skinny old dog.' Henry didn't say it very loudly. 'Go on home.'

The dog sat down at Henry's feet. Henry looked at the dog and the dog looked at Henry.

'I don't think you've got a home. You're

awful thin. Your ribs show right through your skin.'

Thump, thump, thump, replied the tail.

'And you haven't got a collar,' said Henry.

He began to think. If only he could keep the dog! He had always wanted a dog of his very own and now he had found a dog that wanted him. He couldn't go home and leave a hungry dog on the street corner. If only he knew what his mother and father would say! He fingered the two nickels in his pocket. That was it! He would use one of the nickels to phone his mother.

'Come on, Ribsy. Come on, Ribs, old boy. I'm going to call you Ribsy because you're so thin.'

The dog trotted after the boy to the telephone booth in the corner of the drugstore. Henry shoved him into the booth and shut the door. He had never used a pay telephone before. He had to put the telephone book on the floor and stand on tiptoe on it to reach the mouthpiece. He gave the operator his number and dropped his nickel into the coin box.

'Hello — Mum?'

'Why, Henry!' His mother sounded surprised. 'Where are you?'

'At the drugstore near the Y.'

Ribs began to scratch. Thump, thump, thump. Inside the telephone booth the thumps sounded loud and hollow.

'For goodness' sake, Henry, what's that noise?' his mother demanded. Ribs began to whimper and then to howl. 'Henry,' Mrs Huggins shouted, 'are you all right?'

'Yes, I'm all right,' Henry shouted back. He never could understand why his mother always thought something had happened to him when nothing ever did. 'That's just Ribsy.'

'Ribsy?' His mother was exasperated. 'Henry, will you please tell me what is going on?'

'I'm trying to,' said Henry. Ribsy howled louder. People were gathering around the phone booth to see what was going on. 'Mother, I've found a dog, I sure wish I could keep him. He's a good dog and I'd feed him and wash him and everything. Please, Mum.'

'I don't know, dear,' his mother said. 'You'll have to ask your father.'

'Mum!' Henry wailed. 'That's what you always say!' Henry was tired of standing on tiptoe and the phone booth was getting warm. 'Mum, please say yes and I'll never ask for another thing as long as I live!'

'Well, all right, Henry. I guess there isn't any reason why you shouldn't have a dog. But you'll have to bring him home on the bus. Your father has the car today and I can't come after you. Can you manage?'

'Sure! Easy.'

'And Henry, please don't be late. It looks as if it might rain.'

'All right, Mum.' Thump, thump, thump.

'Henry, what's that thumping noise?'

'It's my dog, Ribsy. He's scratching a flea.'

'Oh, Henry,' Mrs Huggins moaned. 'Couldn't you have found a dog without fleas?'

Henry thought that was a good time to hang up. 'Come on, Ribs,' he said. 'We're going home on the bus.'

When the big green bus stopped in front of the drugstore, Henry picked up his dog. Ribsy was heavier than he expected. He had a hard time getting him into the bus and was wondering how he would get a dime out of his pocket when the driver said, 'Say, sonny, you can't take that dog on the bus.'

'Why not?' asked Henry.

'It's a company rule, sonny. No dogs on buses.'

'Golly, Mister, how'm I going to get him home? I just have to get him home.'

'Sorry, sonny. I didn't make the rule. No animal can ride on a bus unless it's inside a box.'

'Well, thanks anyway,' said Henry doubtfully, and lifted Ribsy off the bus.

'Well, I guess we'll have to get a box. I'll get you on to the next bus somehow,' promised Henry.

He went back into the drugstore followed closely by Ribsy. 'Have you got a big box I could have, please?' he asked the man at the toothpaste counter. 'I need one big enough for my dog.'

The clerk leaned over the counter to look at Ribsy. 'A cardboard box?' he asked.

'Yes, please,' said Henry, wishing the man would hurry. He didn't want to be late getting home.

The clerk pulled a box out from under the counter. 'This hair tonic carton is the only one I have. I guess it's big enough, but why anyone would want to put a dog in a cardboard box I can't understand.'

The box was about two feet square and six inches deep. On one end was printed, DON'T LET THEM CALL YOU BALDY, and on the other, TRY OUR LARGE

ECONOMY SIZE.

Henry thanked the clerk, carried the box out to the bus stop, and put it on the sidewalk. Ribsy padded after him. 'Get in, fellow,' Henry commanded. Ribsy understood. He stepped into the box and sat down just as the bus came around the corner. Henry had to kneel to pick up the box.

It was not a very strong box and he had to put his arms under it. He staggered as he lifted it, feeling like the strong man who lifted weights at the circus. Ribsy lovingly licked his face with his wet pink tongue.

'Hey, cut that out!' Henry ordered. 'You better be good if you're going to ride on the bus with me.'

The bus stopped at the kerb. When it was Henry's turn to get on, he had trouble finding the step because he couldn't see his feet. He had to try several times before he hit it. Then he discovered he had forgotten to take his dime out of his pocket. He was afraid to put the box down for fear Ribsy might escape.

He turned sideways to the driver and asked politely, 'Will you please take the dime out of my pocket for me? My hands are full.'

The driver pushed his cap back on his head and exclaimed, 'Full! I should say they *are* full! And just where do you think you're going with that animal?'

'Home,' said Henry in a small voice.

The passengers were staring and most of them were smiling. The box was getting heavier every minute.

'Not on this bus, you're not!' said the driver.

'But the man on the last bus said I could take the dog on the bus in a box,' protested Henry, who was afraid he couldn't hold the dog much longer. 'He said it was a company rule.'

'He meant a big box tied shut. A box with holes punched in it for the dog to breathe through.'

Henry was horrified to hear Ribsy growl. 'Shut up,' he ordered.

Ribsy began to scratch his left ear with his left hind foot. The box began to tear. Ribsy jumped out of the box and off the bus and Henry jumped after him. The bus pulled away with a puff of exhaust.

'Now see what you've done! You've spoiled everything.' The dog hung his head and tucked his tail between his legs. 'If I can't get you home, how can I keep you?'

Henry sat down on the kerb to think. It was so late and the clouds were so dark that he didn't want to waste time looking for a big box. His mother was probably beginning to worry about him.

People were stopping on the corner to wait for the next bus. Among them Henry noticed an elderly lady carrying a large paper shopping bag full of apples. The shopping bag gave him an idea. Jumping up, he snapped his fingers at Ribs and ran back into the drugstore.

'You back again?' asked the toothpaste clerk. 'What do you want this time? String and paper to wrap your dog in?'

'No, sir,' said Henry. 'I want one of those big nickel shopping bags.' He laid his last nickel on the counter.

'Well, I'll be darned,' said the clerk, and handed the bag across the counter.

Henry opened the bag and set it up on the floor. He picked up Ribsy and shoved him hind feet first into the bag. Then he pushed his front feet in. A lot of Ribsy was left over.

The clerk was leaning over the counter watching. 'I guess I'll have to have some string and paper, too,' Henry said, 'if I can have some free.'

'Well! Now I've seen everything.' The clerk shook his head as he handed a piece of string and a big sheet of paper across the counter.

Ribsy whimpered, but he held still while Henry wrapped the paper loosely around his head and shoulders and tied it with the string. The dog made a lumpy package, but by taking one handle of the bag in each hand Henry was able to carry it to the bus stop. He didn't think the bus

driver would notice him. It was getting dark and a crowd of people, most of them with packages, was waiting on the corner. A few spatters of rain hit the pavement.

This time Henry remembered his dime. Both hands were full, so he held the dime in his teeth and stood behind the woman with the bag of apples. Ribsy wiggled and whined, even though Henry tried to pet him through the paper. When the bus stopped, he climbed on behind the lady, quickly set the bag down, dropped his dime in the slot, picked up the bag, and squirmed through the crowd to a seat beside a fat man near the back of the bus.

'Whew!' Henry sighed with relief. The driver was the same one he had met on the first bus! But Ribs was on the bus at last. Now if he could only keep him quiet for fifteen minutes they would be home and Ribsy would be his for keeps.

The next time the bus stopped Henry saw Scooter McCarthy, a fifth grader at school, get on and make his way through the crowd to the back of the bus.

Just my luck, thought Henry. I'll bet he wants to know what's in my bag.

'Hi,' said Scooter.

'Hi,' said Henry.

'Whatcha got in that bag?' asked Scooter.

'None of your beeswax,' answered Henry.

Scooter looked at Henry. Henry looked at Scooter. Crackle, crackle, crackle went the bag. Henry tried to hold it more tightly between his knees.

'There's something alive in that bag!' Scooter said accusingly.

'Shut up, Scooter!' whispered Henry.

'Aw, shut up yourself!' said Scooter. 'You've got something alive in that bag!'

By this time the passengers at the back of the bus were staring at Henry and his package. Crackle, crackle, crackle. Henry tried to pat Ribsy again through the paper. The bag crackled even louder. Then it began to wiggle.

'Come on, tell us what's in the bag,' coaxed the fat man.

'N-n-n-nothing,' stammered Henry. 'Just something I found.'

'Maybe it's a rabbit,' suggested one passenger. 'I think it's kicking.'

'No, it's too big for a rabbit,' said another.

'I'll bet it's a baby,' said Scooter. 'I'll bet you kidnapped a baby!'

'I did not!'

Ribs began to whimper and then to howl. Crackle, crackle, crackle. Thump, thump, thump. Ribsy scratched his way out of the bag.

'Well, I'll be doggonned!' exclaimed the fat man and began to laugh. 'I'll be doggonned!'

'It's just a skinny old dog,' said Scooter.

'He is not! He's a good dog.'

Henry tried to keep Ribsy between his knees. The bus lurched around a corner and started to go uphill. Henry was thrown against the fat man. The frightened dog wiggled away from him, squirmed between the passengers, and started for the front of the bus.

'Here, Ribsy, old boy! Come back here,' called Henry and started after him.

'E-e-ek! A dog!' squealed the lady with the bag of apples. 'Go away, doggie, go away!'

Ribsy was scared. He tried to run and crashed into the lady's bag of apples. The bag tipped over and the apples began to roll toward the back of the bus, which was grinding up a steep hill. The apples rolled around the feet of the people who were standing. Passengers began to slip and slide. They dropped their packages and grabbed one another.

Crash! A high-school girl dropped an armload of books.

Rattle! Bang! Crash! A lady dropped a big paper bag. The bag broke open and pots and pans rolled out.

Thud! A man dropped a coil of garden hose. The hose unrolled and the passengers found it wound around their legs.

People were sitting on the floor. They were sitting on books and apples. They were even sitting on other people's laps.

Some of them had their hats over their faces and their feet in the air.

Scree-e-ech! The driver threw on the brakes and turned around in his seat just as Henry made his way through the apples and books and pans and hose to catch Ribsy.

The driver pushed his cap back on his head. 'OK, sonny,' he said to Henry. 'Now you know why dogs aren't allowed on buses!'

'Yes, sir,' said Henry in a small voice. 'I'm sorry.'

'You're sorry! A lot of good that does. Look at this bus! Look at those people!'

'I didn't mean to make any trouble,' said Henry. 'My mother said I could keep the dog if I could bring him home on the bus.'

The fat man began to snicker. Then he chuckled. Then he laughed and then he roared. He laughed until tears streamed down his cheeks and all the other passengers were laughing too, even the man with the hose and the lady with the apples.

The driver didn't laugh. 'Take that dog and get off the bus!' he ordered. Ribsy whimpered and tucked his tail between his legs.

The fat man stopped laughing. 'See

here, driver,' he said, 'you can't put that boy and his dog off in the rain.'

'Well, he can't stay on the bus,' snapped the driver.

Henry didn't know what he was going to do. He guessed he'd have to walk the rest of the way home. He wasn't sure he knew the way in the dark.

Just then a siren screamed. It grew louder and louder until it stopped right alongside the bus.

A policeman appeared in the entrance. 'Is there a boy called Henry Huggins on this bus?' he asked.

'Oh boy, you're going to be arrested for having a dog on the bus!' gloated Scooter. 'I'll bet you have to go to jail!'

'I'm him,' said Henry in a very small voice.

'I am he,' corrected the lady with the apples, who had been a schoolteacher and couldn't help correcting boys.

'You'd better come along with us,' said the policeman.

'Boy, you're sure going to get it!' said Scooter.

'Surely going to get it,' corrected the apple lady.

Henry and Ribsy followed the policeman off the bus and into the squad car,

119

where Henry and the dog sat in the back seat.

'Are you going to arrest me?' Henry asked timidly.

'Well, I don't know. Do you think you ought to be arrested?'

'No, sir,' said Henry politely. He thought the policeman was joking, but he wasn't sure. It was hard to tell about grown-ups sometimes. 'I didn't mean to do anything. I just had to get Ribsy home. My mother said I could keep him if I could bring him home on the bus.'

'What do you think?' the officer asked his partner, who was driving the squad car.

'We-e-ell, I think we might let him off this time,' answered the driver. 'His mother must be pretty worried about him if she called the police, and I don't think she'd want him to go to jail.'

'Yes, he's late for his dinner already. Let's see how fast we can get him home.'

The driver pushed a button and the siren began to shriek. Ribsy raised his head and howled. The tyres sucked at the wet pavement and the windshield wipers splip-splopped. Henry began to enjoy himself. Wouldn't this be something to tell the kids at school! Automobiles

pulled over to the kerb as the police car
went faster and faster. Even the bus
Henry had been on had to pull over and
stop. Henry waved to the passengers.
They waved back. Up the hill the police
car sped and around the corner until they
came to Klickitat Street and then to
Henry's block and then pulled up in front
of his house.

Henry's mother and father were standing on the porch waiting for him. The
neighbours were looking out of their
windows.

'Well!' said his father after the policeman had gone. 'It's about time you came
home. So this is Ribsy! I've heard about
you, fellow, and there's a big bone and a
can of Feeley's Flea Flakes waiting for
you.'

'Henry, what *will* you do next?' sighed
his mother.

'Golly, Mum, I didn't do anything. I
just brought my dog home on the bus like
you said.'

Ribsy sat down and began to scratch.

Playing with Cuthbert

René Goscinny

I wanted to go out and play with our gang, but Mum said no, nothing doing, she didn't care for the little boys I went around with, we were always up to something silly, and anyway I was invited to tea with Cuthbert, who was a nice little boy with such good manners, and it would be a very good thing if I tried to be more like him.

I wasn't mad keen to go to tea with Cuthbert, or try to be more like him. Cuthbert is top of the class and teacher's pet and a rotten sport but we can't thump him much because of his glasses. I'd rather have gone to the swimming pool with Alec and Geoffrey and Eddie and the rest, but there it was, Mum looked as if she wasn't standing for any nonsense, and anyway I always do what my Mum says especially when she looks as if she isn't standing for any nonsense.

Mum made me wash and comb my hair and told me to put on my blue sailor suit with the nice creases in the trousers, and my white silk shirt and spotted tie. I had to wear that lot for my cousin Angela's wedding, the time I was sick after the reception.

'And don't look like that!' said Mum. 'You'll have a very nice time playing with Cuthbert, I'm sure.' Then we went out. I was scared stiff of meeting the gang. They'd have laughed like a drain to see me got up like that!

Cuthbert's Mum opened the door. 'Oh, isn't he sweet!' she said, and she hugged me and then she called Cuthbert. 'Cuthbert! Come along. Here's your little friend Nicholas.' So Cuthbert came along, he was all dressed up too, with velvet trousers and white socks and funny shiny black sandals. We looked a pair of right Charlies, him and me.

Cuthbert didn't look all that pleased to see me either, he shook my hand and his hand was all limp. 'Well, I'll be off,' said Mum. 'I hope he'll behave, and I'll be back to pick him up at six.' And Cuthbert's Mum said she was sure we'd play nicely and I'd be very good. Mum gave me a rather worried look and then she went away.

We had tea. That was OK, there was chocolate to drink and jam and cake and biscuits and we didn't put our elbows on the table. After tea Cuthbert's Mum told us to go and have a nice game in Cuthbert's room.

Up in his room Cuthbert started by telling me I mustn't thump him because he wore glasses and if I did he'd start to shout about and his Mum would have me put in prison. I told him I'd just love to thump him, but I wasn't going to because I'd promised my Mum to be good. Cuthbert seemed to like the sound of that, and he said right, we'd play. He got out heaps of books: geography books and science books and arithmetic books, and he said we could read and do some sums to pass the time. He told me he knew some brilliant problems about the water from taps running into a bath with the plug pulled out so the bath emptied at the same time as it was filling.

That didn't sound a bad idea, and I asked Cuthbert if I could see his bath because it might be fun. Cuthbert looked at me, took off his glasses, wiped them, thought a minute and then told me to come with him.

There was a big bath in the bathroom and I said why didn't we fill it and sail boats on it? Cuthbert said he'd never thought of that, but it was quite a good idea. The bath didn't take long to fill right up to the top (we put the plug in, not like the problem). But then we were stuck because Cuthbert didn't have any boats to sail in it. He explained that he didn't have many toys at all, he mostly had books. But luckily I can make paper boats and we took some pages out of his arithmetic book. Of course we tried to be careful so that Cuthbert could stick the pages back in the book afterwards, because it's very naughty to harm a book, a tree or a poor dumb animal.

We had a really great time. Cuthbert swished his arm about in the water to make waves. It was a pity he didn't roll up his shirt-sleeves first, and he didn't take off the watch he got for coming first in the last history test we had and now it says twenty past four all the time. After a bit longer, I don't know just how much longer because of the watch not working, we'd had enough of playing boats. Anyway there was water all over the place and we didn't want to make too much mess because there were muddy puddles on the floor and Cuthbert's sandals weren't as shiny as they used to be.

We went back to Cuthbert's room and he showed me his globe, which is a big metal ball on a stand with seas and continents and things on it. Cuthbert explained that it was for learning geography and finding where the different countries were. I knew that already, there's a globe like that at school and our teacher showed us how it works. Cuthbert told me you could unscrew his globe, and then it was like a big ball. I think it was me that got the idea of playing ball with it, only that turned out not to be such a very good idea after all. We did have some fun throwing and catching the globe, but Cuthbert had taken off his glasses so as not to risk breaking them, and he doesn't see very well without his glasses, so he missed the globe and the part with Australia on it hit his mirror and the mirror got broken. Cuthbert put his glasses on again to see what had happened and he was very upset. We put the globe back on its stand and decided to be more careful in case our Mums weren't too pleased.

So we looked for something else to do, and Cuthbert told me his Dad had given him a chemistry set to help him with science. He showed me the chemistry set; it's brilliant. It's a big box full of tubes and funny round bottles and little flasks full of things all different colours, and a

spirit burner too. Cuthbert told me you could do some very instructive experiments with this chemistry set.

He started pouring little bits of powder and liquid into the tubes and they changed colour and went red or blue and now and then there was a puff of white smoke. It was ever so instructive. I told Cuthbert we ought to try something even more instructive, and he agreed. We took the biggest bottle and tipped all the powders and liquids into it and then we got the spirit burner and heated up the bottle. It was OK to start with; the stuff began frothing up, and then there was some very black smoke. The trouble was the smoke didn't smell too good and it made everything very dirty. When the bottle burst we had to stop the experiment.

Cuthbert started howling that he couldn't see any more, but luckily it was only because the lenses of his glasses were all black, and while he wiped them I opened the window, because the smoke was making us cough. And the froth was making funny noises on the carpet, like boiling water, and the walls were all black and we weren't terribly clean ourselves.

Then Cuthbert's Mum came in. For a moment she didn't say anything at all, just opened her eyes and her mouth very wide, and then she started to shout, she took off Cuthbert's glasses and she slapped him, and then she led us off to the bathroom to get washed. When Cuthbert's Mum saw the bathroom she wasn't too pleased about that either.

Cuthbert was hanging on to his glasses for dear life, so as not to get slapped again. Cuthbert's Mum went off telling me she was going to ring my mother and ask her to come and fetch me immediately and she'd never seen anything like it in all her born days and it was absolutely incredible.

Mum did come to fetch me pretty soon, and I was pleased, because I wasn't having so much fun at Cuthbert's house any more, not with his Mum carrying on like that. Mum took me home, telling me all the way she supposed I was proud of myself and I wouldn't have any pudding this evening. I must say, that was fair enough, because we did do one or two daft things at Cuthbert's. And actually Mum was right, as usual: I *did* have a nice time playing with Cuthbert. I'd have liked to go and see him again, but it seems that Cuthbert's Mum doesn't want him to be friends with me.

Honestly, mothers! I do wish they could make up their minds, you just don't know *who* to play with!

The Kidnapping

Catherine Storr

One day Polly was in the kitchen, washing up dreamily at the sink. Outside the sun was shining hot and bright, and a delicious smell of newly-cut grass came in through the open window. Bert, the odd job man, was piling up the grass cuttings in a corner of the garden to make a compost heap; Lucy, Polly's little sister, was helping him, or thought she was helping, by carrying small piles of grass to and fro, sometimes in the right direction, but more often in the wrong one.

'Bert,' said a voice from the other side

of the house. 'Bert! Come here a minute, will you?'

'Wharris'it?' Bert called back: but he went on piling up his compost heap.

'See you about something very important!' the voice said urgently.

Polly could see Bert say Bother: she couldn't hear it, but the way he put down the rake showed exactly how he was feeling. Then he went off along the path in the direction of the voice. Lucy, alone in the back garden, filled a small tin pail with gravel and wandered over the lawn, sprinkling it with little stones.

Suddenly a large black Something jumped over the garden wall, snatched up Lucy and was off again before Polly had quite realized what was happening. But she knew directly who it had been. Only the wolf would come into the garden like that and steal small fat Lucy. For what? It was a horrible thought.

For the first time in all her dealings with the wolf, Polly was frightened. But she knew she must do something quickly, so she ran out of the kitchen, without even waiting to dry her hands, out through the garden and into the hot dusty road outside.

She looked up and down, but there was

no one in sight. A scatter of small pebbles led off to the right.

'He must have gone home,' Polly thought. 'He wouldn't take Lucy anywhere she'd be recognized, it wouldn't be safe for him.'

The pebbles led in the direction of the wolf's house. Polly had never gone that way alone before, and she didn't much like doing it now, but the thought of Lucy in the wolf's power drove her on.

Outside the wolf's door she stopped. She wasn't sure how she was going to get Lucy out; she had no plans and she didn't want to have to go into the house herself. She put up her hand to ring the door-bell; then she took it down again. She actually lifted the knocker, but let it fall back silently. Polly, for once, was at a loss.

She was just summoning her courage to let the wolf know she had arrived, when something went hurtling past her head. Someone inside the house had thrown a stick out of the window just beside the porch, and it had only just missed hitting her in the face. A moment later a large black body followed the stick out of the window. The wolf retrieved the stick and jumped neatly back through the window again.

'Good dog,' Polly heard Lucy's voice saying, 'fetch stick.'

'I'm not a dog, you silly little girl,' the wolf's voice said crossly. 'I'm a wolf, and I'm going to —'

'More,' said Lucy. She always said more for something she had enjoyed the first time — more cake, more dance, more Red Riding Hood. The stick flew out of the window again, this time further from Polly's head.

'Fetch stick! Good dog!'

The wolf came, rather more slowly, out of the window and went back again with the stick in his mouth.

'Clever dog,' Lucy said approvingly.

'You're stupid,' the wolf said, really annoyed. 'You're almost as stupid as Polly. Listen, stupid little Lucy, I'm NOT a dog. I'm a wolf, and I'm going to eat you all up.'

'Good wolf,' said Lucy contentedly. 'Fetch stick.'

For the third time the stick came out and was fetched by a reluctant and now definitely sulky wolf. As he landed inside the room again, he turned and slammed the bottom of the window down hard.

'Now you can't throw the stick out again,' he said. 'You can't reach up to the top opening. Now do listen properly, Lucy. I am not a dog, do you understand?'

'Not dog,' said Lucy agreeably.

Polly moved up to the window and peered in. It was not a very comfortable-looking room, a sort of parlour, furnished stiffly and scantily, with hard knobbly-looking chairs and a shiny horsechair sofa. A large dog-basket containing a piece of striped blanket near the fireplace seemed to indicate that the wolf some-times slept here; there was a round table in the middle of the room, partly covered by a red woollen crochet mat.

Lucy was sitting comfortably in the dog-basket. She had discovered a hole in the stripy blanket and she was picking at the edges and enlarging it with apparent satisfaction. The wolf was sitting at the table, looking annoyed, tapping on the table, biting his nails, and showing every sign of being anxious and jumpy.

'I am NOT a dog, Lucy,' he said again, impressively.

Lucy took no notice of this remark.

'I am a wolf.'

'Wolf,' Lucy agreed. She stuck her thumb through the hole in the blanket and said, 'Look! Thumb!'

'I am a wolf and I'm going to eat you all up.'

This was a game with which Lucy was quite familiar. She climbed out of the basket and approached the wolf with her mouth wide open.

'Eat you all up,' she repeated, and, reaching the wolf, sank her small sharp teeth into his front left leg.

'Ow! Wow!' the wolf said indignantly, pulling away from her sharply, 'don't do that! It hurts, you horrible little creature!' He nursed his wounded limb tenderly with the other paw and looked at Lucy in hurt surprise.

But Lucy was delighted. She had seldom had a playfellow who acted pain

and surprise so well, and she was encouraged to improve on her efforts. She walked round behind the wolf, saw his irresistible feathery tail hanging out between the bars of the chair, and gave it a sharp pull.

The wolf turned round with a yelp of astonishment and pain.

'Eat you all up,' said Lucy, opening her mouth at him again and laughing heartily. She made another successful snap at his other front paw.

'You beastly little girl,' the wolf said, now nearly in tears. 'You don't understand the simplest remark. I didn't bring you here to bite me and pull my tail and make me do stupid, useless things like jumping in and out of windows to fetch your horrid stick as if I were a tame dog. Can't you see it isn't you that's going to eat me up, it's me that is going to eat you up? Now. For my lunch. No,' he added, looking at the marble pillared clock on the mantelpiece, which permanently told the time of a quarter past four. 'For my tea.'

'Tea,' said Lucy. She was rather like an echo sometimes, picking on the one familiar word out of a long speech. 'Lucy's tea.'

'Not for you,' the wolf said firmly.

'*Tea*,' said Lucy, equally firmly and a good deal louder.

'No tea for you. For me,' the wolf explained.

'*Tea*,' said Lucy at the top of her voice. Her face suddenly grew brick red and her mouth went square. An enormous tear rolled down her cheek and made a considerable pool on the oilcloth floor.

'Don't cry!' the wolf said, alarmed. 'For goodness' sake don't cry. And don't shriek. Someone might hear, and anyhow I can't bear children who cry, it makes me go funny all over.'

'Tea,' Lucy said, in a quieter voice, but the wolf recognized the dangers of delay.

'Yes, yes,' he said soothingly, 'tea for Lucy.'

'Lucy's chair,' said Lucy, climbing up and sitting on it expectantly. No more tears appeared, and her colour was miraculously restored to normal.

'That's the chair I always sit on,' the wolf complained.

'*Lucy's chair*,' Lucy said: her colour began to rise alarmingly, and her mouth began to set into corners.

'Yes, yes, Lucy's chair.' The wolf pulled a sort of cross-legged stool up to the table and sat on it, trying to look as if he were enjoying himself.

'Butter,' Lucy demanded.

The wolf slipped off his stool and disappeared out of the door. When he came back a minute or two later, he was carrying a tray on which he seemed to have loaded everything he could think of that Lucy could possibly want for tea. There was a large brown steaming teapot, a rusty battered kettle, a sugar bowl, a chipped mug with a picture of an engine on it, a cocoa tin with no lid, half full of biscuits, a plastic plate, the end of a brown loaf, and a sizeable piece of butter in a green soap dish. He put the tray on the table and looked at Lucy nervously.

'Tea,' said Lucy approvingly. She leant forward and seized the mug, looked into it, found it empty, and held it out to the wolf.

'Tea,' she said again. 'Lucy's tea.
Butter.'

The wolf hastily picked up the teapot in
a paw that trembled slightly and tipped it
to pour into the mug. But when Lucy saw
the colour of the liquid that came out of
the spout, her face changed.

'Tea!' she said in disgust. 'No tea.
Milk!'

She took the mug away just before the
wolf removed the teapot. A stream of
nearly boiling tea cascaded down to the
floor and splashed on his foot.

'Ow! That hurts! You've made me
hurt my foot,' he cried reproachfully. But
Lucy was not interested in the wolf's
troubles.

'*Milk*,' was all she said, but the wolf
knew better now than to delay. He left the
room and was back again with a jug of
milk quicker than Polly would have

believed possible. He filled Lucy's mug, and she drank thirstily, and then held out the mug again for more.

'But this is all I've got,' the wolf pleaded. 'The milkman doesn't call again until tomorrow, and I meant to make a milk pudding for supper.'

'*More milk*,' Lucy said.

'I'll just keep enough to put in my tea,' the wolf said, apologetically, pouring out about half the mugful.

'*More*,' said Lucy. 'Lucy thirsty,' she explained in a friendly way, as she drained the last remnants of the unfortunate wolf's milk supply. She looked round the table for further replenishment. 'Butter.'

The wolf, obviously at the end of his resources, pushed the soap dish towards her. Lucy frowned.

'Bread 'n' butter,' she said, clearly pitying anyone who did not understand the simplest rules of behaviour.

The wolf cut a large slice of bread and spread it with a moderate supply of butter. Lucy took it, and began to lick the butter. The wolf stared at her in horror. He sat in a stupefied silence till Lucy, having licked the bread quite dry of its butter, held it out to him and said emphatically, 'More.'

143

'More?' said the wolf. He could hardly believe his ears.

'More butter,' said Lucy impatiently.

'But you haven't eaten the bread. I mean to say, people don't just go on having more butter on the same piece of bread. That isn't what bread and butter means,' the wolf protested.

'*More butter.*'

'Oh, very well. Have it your own way.' The wolf spread a generous layer of butter on the slice of bread and handed it back to Lucy.

He poured himself out a cup of bitter black tea. There was no milk left, so he sweetened it liberally with sugar, and began to drink, making a face as he tasted how nasty it was. But Lucy had noticed his last action and had had a new idea.

'Sugar,' she said, dropping her bread, now licked nearly clean again, on the floor. She held out her hand for the sugar basin.

'No,' said the wolf, with unusual firmness. 'I'm not going to let you polish off all my sugar.' He hid the sugar basin behind him, on his stool. 'Have a biscuit?' He held the cocoa tin out towards Lucy.

Lucy looked doubtfully into the tin.

'Choc bikkit?' she inquired.

'No — o — but there's a very nice one here. Look!' and the wolf held up a crumbling Oval Osborne.

'No bikkit,' said Lucy.

'Nice biscuit,' said the wolf.

'No bikkit.'

'No, no. Certainly. It's a repellent biscuit,' the wolf said, putting it back in the cocoa tin. 'You don't want a nasty biscuit like that. I'll find you a really good biscuit this time.'

He scrabbled busily about at the bottom of the tin, then produced the same biscuit and held it out to Lucy invitingly.

'Sugar,' said Lucy.

'No,' said the wolf.

'*Sugar*.'

'No.'

Lucy abandoned this unprofitable conversation and looked round the room for inspiration.

'Lucy have an apple?' she asked politely.

'I haven't got any apples,' the wolf replied.

'Banana?'

'I haven't any bananas.'

'Then I have bun,' Lucy said decisively. She was sure there could be no one who couldn't produce at least a bun, even if they were so unfortunate as not to have apples and bananas.

'I haven't got —' the wolf began, but he changed his mind. He was reluctantly learning a little cunning too. He looked into the biscuit tin for the third time and gave a start of well-acted surprise.

'Why, what's this?' he cried, 'I was just going to say I hadn't got any buns, but there's one left at the bottom of the tin.'

He held the Oval Osborne biscuit out to Lucy in a trembling paw. She gave him an enchanting smile and took it.

'Gank you.'

It seemed to Polly that this was the moment to ring the front door bell. She pressed it firmly, and kept her finger there for some time.

The door was opened abruptly. An exhausted, frayed wolf, visibly at his last resources, stood before her.

'Polly!' he said. 'You've come in the nick of time. Another five minutes and I don't know what I should have done. For goodness' sake come in and take her away before she eats up everything I've got in the house. Do you know,' he went on, trembling with rage, as he led the way from the front door to the room where Lucy was finishing her biscuit, 'that she even tried to eat me?'

Lucy was sitting comfortably and crumbily on the wolf's special chair when Polly came into the room. She looked at Polly without any special surprise and said agreeably, 'Good morning, Polly.' She always said, 'Good morning,' whatever the time of the day, finding it easier to pronounce than 'Good afternoon.'

'I've come to take you home,' Polly said. She had decided to pretend that the whole affair had been carried on under the politest circumstances. 'Get down from your chair, Lucy, and thank the kind wolf for asking you to tea.'

Lucy obediently struggled off the chair and made for the door as fast as she could.

'Say thank you,' Polly reminded her as they reached the front door again.

'Gank you, Wolf,' Lucy said, 'Lucy come back soon.'

'Not too soon,' the wolf pleaded. He looked very limp as he held the door open for them to go out.

'And now,' Lucy said, as, holding Polly's hand she trotted down the short garden path. 'Lucy go home and have *tea*.'

Behind her Polly heard the wolf groan. He had at last met his match.

Me and the Tooth-Fairy

Chris Powling

Have you ever met the tooth-fairy? I
haven't. Nor has any other kid, so far as I
know. Yet the tooth-fairy must be real
because who else would sneak into your
room after dark and swop your tooth for a
ten-pence piece? And who else would
make your tooth go wobbly in the first
place? A tooth-fairy is the only explana-
tion. It stands to reason.

So, when my very first tooth was about
to fall out, I started to ask questions.
'What does the tooth-fairy look like?' I
said.

'Like a bumble bee,' said Mum. 'With a money-bag instead of a sting.'

'Like a tiny Santa Claus,' said Dad. 'Only with the beard and the reindeer missing.'

'Like a goblin,' said my Big Brother. 'That tooth of yours wouldn't be loose in the first place if you hadn't been goblin' your breakfast, goblin' your dinner and goblin' your tea.'

'Very funny,' I said.

But all the same I couldn't help wondering. Was the tooth-fairy like a butterfly? Or a grasshopper? Or a humming-bird? My favourite idea was the humming-bird. I imagined the tooth-fairy hovering by my bed in a buzz of wings while it shifted the tooth from under my pillow bit by bit. He'd brighten up the night like a firework.

He? Who said the tooth-fairy was a he? The tooth-fairy was so secret I wasn't even sure if it was a boy or a girl who would bring me my ten-pence piece.

Two days later my wobbly tooth plopped into my cornflakes. 'Now you're a gappy kid,' said Mum.

'Now I'll meet the tooth-fairy,' I said.

'You won't,' Dad smiled.

'Why not?'

'Because the tooth-fairy only comes if

you're asleep. A stay-awake kid means a stay-away tooth-fairy.'

'Is that true?'

'True as toast,' said my Big Brother. 'And don't think you can fool the tooth-fairy, either. The tooth-fairy can always tell a fake snore from a proper snore.'

This made me really fed up. How could I snoop and snooze at the same time? It was impossible. The tooth-fairy would stay a secret for ever and there was nothing I could do about it. Or was there?

I began to think hard. What I needed was something to stop the tooth-fairy getting away afterwards. What I needed was . . . a tooth-fairy trap. Yes!

For the rest of the day I worked non-stop. It wasn't easy to build the world's first tooth-fairy trap. Here's what I had to use:

An umbrella
Elastic
A birdcage
Two walking-sticks
Glue
Three coat-hangers bent out of shape
Vinegar and brown paper
An old fishing-rod
My tooth

Soon the trap was ready. 'Keep well away from my room,' I told Mum and Dad and my Big Brother. 'I'm setting up a surprise for the tooth-fairy.'

'What sort of surprise?' they asked.

'Shush,' I answered. 'In case the tooth-fairy gets to hear about it.'

That night, before I snuggled up in bed, I wrote a note in my very best capital letters. It said,

SORRY ABOUT THE TRAP IT'S YOUR
OWN FAULT FOR TRYING TO TRICK A
NIFTY PERSON LIKE ME

Then I put the note and my tooth under the pillow and switched off the light.

I went to sleep at once. Straightaway I started to dream: I dreamt of bats and

152